An Inquirer's Guide to Christian Believing

Answering questions of belief
with a "Yes *and* no
(and I *don't* mean maybe!)"

An Inquirer's Guide to Christian Believing

Answering questions of belief
with a "Yes *and* no
(and I *don't* mean maybe!)"

GUNNAR URANG

Wipf & Stock Publishers
Eugene, Oregon

Wipf & Stock Publishers
199 West 8th Avenue, Suite 3
Eugene, OR 97401

An Inquirer's Guide to Christian Believing
Answering questions of belief with a "Yes and *no (and I* don't *mean maybe!)"*

ISBN: 1-59752-058-6
Publication Date: January 2005

10 9 8 7 6 5 4 3 2 1

ACKNOWLEDGMENTS

Grateful acknowledgment is made to the following for permission to reprint previously published material:

Excerpts from COLLECTED POEMS 1909-1962 by T. S. Eliot, copyright 1936 by Harcourt, Inc., copyright © 1964, 1963 by T. S. Eliot, reprinted by permission of the publisher.

From AMERICAN PRIMITIVE by Mary Oliver. Copyright © 1978, 1979, 1980, 1981, 1982, 1983 by Mary Oliver; first appeared in YANKEE MAGAZINE. By permission of Little, Brown and Company (Inc.).

"Red Geranium and Godly Mignonette" by D. H. Lawrence, from THE COMPLETE POEMS OF D. H. LAWRENCE by D. H. Lawrence, edited by V. de Sola Pinto & F. W. Roberts, copyright © 1964, 1971 by Angelo Ravagli and C. M. Weekley, Executors of the Estate of Frieda Lawrence Ravagli. Used by permission of Viking Penguin, a division of Penguin Putnam Inc.

"Du siehst, ich will viel . . . / You see, I want a . . ." by Rainer Maria Rilke, translated by Anita Barrows & Joanna Macy, from RILKE'S BOOK OF HOURS: LOVE POEMS TO GOD by Rainer Maria Rilke, translated by Anita Barrows and Joanna Macy, copyright © 1996 by Anita Barrows and Joanna Macy. Used by permission of Riverhead Books, a division of Penguin Putnam, Inc.

Citations from the Bible, unless otherwise noted, are from the NEW REVISED STANDARD VERSION of the Bible, copyright © 1989 by the Division of Christian Education of the National Council of Churches of Christ in the U.S.A. Used by permission.

BRING MANY NAMES
Words: Brian Wren
© 1989 Hope Publishing Co., Carol Stream, IL 60188. All rights reserved. Used by permission.

JESU, JESU, FILL US WITH YOUR LOVE
Words: Tom Colvin
© 1969 Hope Publishing Co., Carol Stream, IL 606188. All rights reserved. Used by permission.

THE CHURCH OF CHRIST IN EVERY AGE
Words by Fred Pratt Green
© 1971 Hope Publishing Co., Carol Stream, IL 50188. All rights reserved. Used by permission.

For Sarah

CONTENTS

PREFACE

This is a book filled with echoes. Echoes of questions raised—or implied—by voices heard through the years in living rooms and kitchens, in coffee places, in classrooms, in church gatherings.

> *"If God is all-powerful and all-loving, why do such terrible things happen to people?": the voice of a perplexed student, echoing without realizing it the classic, agelong question concerning the "problem of evil."*
>
> *"What I want to know"—the voice of a medical researcher in a church study group—"is why Jesus had to die."*
>
> *The voice of an older, longtime churchgoer commenting to the preacher after a carefully-thought-out sermon grappling with the myth-imbued creation stories of Genesis: "It sounds to me like you don't believe the Bible."*
>
> *My own voice challenging one of my divinity school theology professors: "But what is the authority undergirding your structure of beliefs? On what do they rest?"*
>
> *The voice of a young child, after the death of a beloved, grandfatherly friend of the family (the silent question in the spoken affirmation): "We'll see him again, at the resurrection."*

Echoes of affirmations made, as well, then—by others sitting at kitchen tables or in restaurant booths or in discussion circles. And of the resources informing those statements of belief, resources such as these, so important to the shape of my own questioning and response:

> *Voices from Scripture, since I, like the Apostle Paul's*

colleague Timothy, have "from childhood known the sacred writings" (2 Timothy 3:15)—the stories, sayings, and "picture thinking" of the Bible.

Voices of classroom instructors in theology and related fields of study, as well as in (from earlier times) language and literature.

The voice of the mind's dialogue with the authors of those readings making up the continuing-education curriculum of a lifelong learner and teacher.

The voices, already referred to, from conversations and colloquies in which I have been participant or leader and for which the venue has shifted (following ordination) from the academic scene to predominantly church settings.

And the voice within that never stops reflecting on day-to-day experiences as family member, citizen, worker, and (in all these things) child of God.

In one sense, therefore, this book simply continues the conversation, recollecting the questions that won't go away and re-collecting resources for attempting responses to them. Specifically, it continues that part of the conversation carried on with persons perplexed by issues of belief but feeling, often, that they lack the access to theological discourse seemingly required for exploring them.

For each major question of belief taken up, then, I have attempted to listen for the voices of Holy Scripture, to collect and re-collect relevant insights from theologians, and to set out my own coherent statement of the question itself and of answers that might be ventured—all in language intended to be clear and non-technical and to reach across denominational lines.

What is problematic in the answering of such questions is signalled by the invitation to a "yes" and "no" response. The "yes" or "no" emerges according to what point of view is entered into or what interpretation of the biblical texts is embraced. Take, for example, the question "Is the Bible the 'Word of God'?": there are perspectives from which part of the answer has to be "no" and interpretations whereby a strong "yes" can also be affirmed.

The "and I *don't* mean maybe!" is meant to convey an essential assurance: that reflecting on the problems involved in holding a particular *belief about* God need not weaken the fully committed *faith in* God of which beliefs are a component. The Bible functions best as "Word of God"—to stay with the question from Chapter Two—for those who know it to be also, and at the same time, a thoroughly *human* word.

In writing a book to continue the conversation about belief carried on for so many years, I have incurred great debts to the many conversation partners along the way. There are my teachers, those whose voices have reached my mind and heart in classroom settings and by way of books and articles written. Faculty and clergy colleagues, as well. And students, at the colleges where I have taught, who—voicing their perplexity or dogmatic assurance or withering skepticism—have taught me much about belief (and healthy disbelief!). The church folk, finally—in Middlebury, Rutland, Springfield, Proctorsville, and Norwich, Vermont (as well as those from various parts of the state in Vermont's Diocesan Study Program)—who have so patiently listened to my speaking and so helpfully voiced their own convictions and misgivings.

Special appreciation is due those who tuned in to the voice behind the book in its various manuscript stages. These include: my editor at Wipf and Stock, Jim Tedrick; those persons—such as June Schulte, Mary Young, family members John and Alison and Sally, and Bishop (retired) Arthur Walmsley—who read parts of earlier versions; and Burton Cooper, theologian, teacher, writer—and sometime colleague—who read the entire manuscript and, with the right mixture of receptivity and resistance, offered numerous suggestions for correcting or clarifying its line of thought.

The one, especially, to whom the book is dedicated—honored here as well as on the dedication page, because besides being the one with whom I have explored, in love and comradeship, what Wendell Berry speaks of as "the country of marriage" she has also been partner in a continuous conversation that can be overheard on many pages of this book and that continues to enliven and enrich all my days.

INTRODUCTION

Does It Matter What We Believe?

Do beliefs matter? For some in our time—Islamic fundamentalists, Christian Zionists, certain upholders of "moral values"—beliefs seem to matter all too much. And yet, compared with times past, when for most people the answer to that question would have been an unhesitating yes, a surprising number today would want to say no.

"No," some of these would say, "I'm spiritual, but I'm not religious." Or: "Belief is 'head' stuff; my concern is not head but heart." Or: "What we need is right thinking and right action in the world; insistence on right belief seems to cause nothing but conflict and violence."

It sounds as if for people like this it's a matter of faith versus belief. Faith has to do with our whole being. It is "an opening of the heart," says Alan Jones, "to all of reality,"[1] and it is revealed in the way we "lean into" one way of existing rather than another. Some people rest in a reality that can be spoken of as "God" to give meaning and purpose to our world and our individual existence in it. Others hold to a "secular" faith, and rely on the capabilities of human beings ("Have faith in yourself") and on the "natural" processes of the cosmos.

When we act habitually on any such leaning—choosing this line of work rather than that, deciding that certain actions are right and others wrong, planning our work and play and rest, continuing a life effort even after severe disappointment—we are living by our "faith."

But such faith can never be separated from belief, even if the particular beliefs held are under the radar of awareness. Ask a friend, "Why do you discipline your child in that way?" Her next sentence is likely to begin, "Because I believe . . . ." Ask why a co-worker attends church. He is likely to respond, "Because I believe . . . ." And note that the answer will take the same form if the question is: "Why *don't* you go to church?"

"Because I believe." As human beings, we can't keep from asking questions about ourselves and our world, among them those questions in which we find ourselves asking "Why?"—asking, with what theologian Paul Tillich called "ultimate concern," "Why?"

Why do such terrible things happen in the world? Why has such devastation come into *my* life? Why do such *wonderful* things happen? What does it mean that a sudden glimpse of a white-tailed deer or an outburst of birdsong can make my heart turn over, or that a few words in a song or at the end of a movie can cause my throat to tighten and tears to come to my eyes? Why—to what purpose—am I working so hard and centering such attention on the people or projects in my life? Why am I able to love and how is it that I could be worthy of being beloved? Or, why do I remain so self-absorbed and find it so hard to reach out to others? Why do I feel so strongly about the unfairness of things, and the misery so many people have to suffer? And why am I unable to rid myself of the fear of dying?

When pushed far enough, such questions turn out to be about basic trust, or the lack of it. Do I live my life—loving, working, playing, thinking, serving—within a "faith" that reality tends toward love that is reciprocated, work that has value, play that gives real pleasure, thinking that yields truth, and service that makes a difference? When the questioning takes us deeper yet, so that we find ourselves asking what could be the *ground* for a reality so infused with value, pleasure, truth, justice, and love, we are approaching God-talk.

But the motions of the spirit by which we seek to respond in faith can seem at odds with what the mind holds as beliefs. In one respect, faith and belief are always at odds. No one *could* ever state fully in terms of belief all that is present in the dispositions, feelings, and actions of a lived faith. Questions about God are questions about ultimate mystery; answers given to those questions must always be mere gropings in that mystery.

More specifically, circumstances in our lives may seem to contradict previously-held understandings of the relationship between God and humankind. C. S. Lewis was a staunch defender of what he identified as "mere Christianity." Yet, in the time of grieving after the death of his wife, he was described as "a man who still believes in God but cannot find evidence for his goodness."[2]

It can also happen that certain declarations of belief are felt to *misrepresent* our walk with God. Or the way such beliefs are *held* can be at odds with our own experience of divine presence and violate the personal freedom true faith insists on. Some get their backs up when expected, like Alice's Queen, in *Through the Looking Glass*, to "believe as many as six impossible things before breakfast"! Or to stand with "true believers" who seem more driven by fear and loathing than inspired by faith and love.

One purpose for this book, therefore, is to help illumine the thinking that is already going on in response to the continuous questioning at the heart of human existence. Any of us undergoing a "belief debriefing" would discover, perhaps to our amazement, how many elements of a "creed" even a seemingly unreligious person has partially worked through. The book also seeks to clarify some of the major beliefs in the Christian tradition that has been so important in the history of European and American culture and so influential in other parts of the world.

The answers considered—the answers *questioned*, one could say—include some that have come to be seen as especially problematic and, therefore, controversial. It is particularly important to address responsibly any beliefs that may have become stumbling-blocks to a relationship with God—and with fellow human beings.

Sometimes a particular belief is simply found unsatisfactory: the idea that suffering has to be divine punishment for human sins, for example, or that everything in the Bible has to be taken as fact. But also—surprisingly, perhaps—the equally wrong ideas that humans are *not* sinners, or that Jesus was not "God-with-us" but only an especially "good guy" whose teachings we need to take seriously in our own moral endeavors.

Sometimes what offends are taken-for-granted beliefs within the book Christians accept as "holy scripture." Such assumptions can be detected, for instance, in the prevalence of masculine language with reference to God, or imagery presenting God as king, or characterizations of God as warlord seemingly issuing orders for genocide. What needs to be insisted on in such cases is that to be a "Bible-believing Christian" is not to "*believe in*" the Bible; it is to believe in the God we come to know *by way of* the Bible.

Living by a biblical faith requires of us a "yes," a "yes" to the God continuously present to us within the life opportunities continuously offered us. Questions of *belief*, in contrast, require a "yes *and* no." "Genuine faith," declares Brother David Steindl-Rast, "holds its beliefs firmly, yes, but ever so lightly."[3]

Can we say "yes *and* no" to beliefs and "yes and I *don't* mean maybe!" to faith?

This is our predicament, then: We can't be content to float along without reflecting at all; humans are creatures that think. Nor can we mouth uncritically the answers we have been given by other people; humans need to be free to think for themselves. At the same time, it is not helpful, either, to insist on clear, simple answers to questions that reach into the heart of inexhaustible mystery—especially if we then want to banish those who can't agree with our formulations! No, what is asked of us in our wrestling with such issues of faith and belief is something that many find difficult—that we learn, in the words of the twentieth-century German poet Rainer Maria Rilke, to "love the questions."

We keep answering "yes *and* no" to these questions about God and us because we are aware of our own limited, even distorted, capacity for comprehending mystery. And because, as the great physicist Niels Bohr is reported to have said, "A deep truth is a true statement whose opposite is also true."[4]

And the "I *don't* mean maybe!"? This has to do with the intensity in our questioning. Our ultimate concern, after all, is living a relationship in which we know ourselves not just as those who ask questions but as those who *are* the question, and seek to know God not just as the one who gives answers but the one who *is* the answer.

The questioning and answering going on in our individual inner conversations about God and in our less frequent (not nearly frequent enough!) conversations with other people on religious matters is important not for its own sake but in so far as it helps us maintain that relationship. For in that connection all that is meant by the word "salvation" is happening—self-acceptance, forgiveness, deliverance, peace, communion, joy, celebration, efforts in behalf of justice and peace—for us as individuals and, through us, to others near at hand and across the world with the same questioning minds and the same needy hearts.

> "So many are alive," says the poet Rilke,
>
> who don't seem to care.
> Casual, easy, they move in the world
> as though untouched.
> But you take pleasure in the faces
> of those who know they thirst.
> You cherish those
> who grip you for survival.[5]

This book consists, then, of a series of questions about basic Christian beliefs the answers to which have been, and continue to be, controversial. Each chapter will try to make clear why the answer to its particular question has to be a "yes *and* no" and how the response can also include, nevertheless, an emphatic "And I *don't* mean maybe!"

For those with some knowledge of Christianity but finding themselves confused about certain beliefs they have been led to identify as Christian, this book can provide a greater clarity in their understanding of this familiar yet strange religion—thus addressing, perhaps, what pollster George Gallup, Jr., identifies as the "knowledge gap" in the religious experience of Americans: "the often vast difference between Americans' stated faith and their lack of the most basic knowledge about that faith."[6] Non-Christians may find in this book a useful survey of Christian belief presented in nontechnical style and noncoercive rhetoric.

What a book like this one is meant to make possible is suggested by a conversation, in the novel *Absolute Truths*, by the British writer Susan Howatch, between an English bishop and an American woman acquaintance. The woman is explaining how it is that, after years of indifference to things religious, she came to find herself reading about the Christian faith and, eventually, attending church.

First, she tells her clerical friend, she arrived at the realization that in her neglect she had been overlooking "two thousand years of accumulated wisdom about the most vital issues of life." Then it came to her—and this is why the reading program was undertaken—that

> "a good religion resembles a language—it can be spoken by adults and children alike, by the uneducated and the educated, the geniuses and the morons, and like all languages it's powered by metaphor, symbol, and analogy . . . ."

It's a language, furthermore, which expresses "complex and profound" truths, beyond the boundaries drawn by many contemporary thinkers.

Thus it was that she started reading about the Christian religion "in order to acquire the basic skills in this new language." As for churchgoing—that came, she says, because "in order to gain fluency [in this new language, she] needed to go to a place where the language was regularly spoken."[7]

This book offers something of a survey of that "accumulated wisdom about the most vital issues of life." It offers a way whereby we who, somehow, believe but also feel the need for help with our unbelief can deal honestly with questions about the "complex and profound" truths expressed in the language of Christian belief. It offers an invitation, as well, perhaps, to continue going to—or start looking for—"a place where the language [is] regularly spoken."

ENDNOTES

[1] Alan Jones, *The Soul's Journey: Exploring the Three Passages of the Spiritual Life with Dante as a Guide* (HarperSanFrancisco, 1995), 134.

[2] A. N. Wilson, *C. S. Lewis: A Biography* (New York: W. W. Norton and Co., 1990), 284.
[3] Brother David Steindl-Rast, *Gratefulness, the Heart of Prayer: An Approach to Life in Fullness* (New York: Paulist Press, 1984), 98.
[4] Reference in Lewis Thomas, *Late Night Thoughts on Listening to Mahler's Ninth Symphony* (New York: Viking Press, 1983), 23.
[5] Rainer Maria Rilke, *Rilke's Book of Hours: Love Poems to God*, trans. Anita Barrows and Joanna Macy (New York, Riverhead Books, 1996), 61.
[6] "Gaps," in *Anglican Digest* (Pentecost, 1997), 9.
[7] Susan Howatch, *Absolute Truths* (New York, Alfred A. Knopf, 1995), 271.

CHAPTER ONE

Can We Know God?
Questions about God as Self-Revealing Mystery

We who try to think about God—what are we thinking *about*? We who want to know God—what are we looking for? We who are Christian believers in God—what does Jesus have to do with all this?

We are thinking, first of all, about the world as mystery, about a "beyondness" in and under and around everything that is. We want to know that mystery as present to us and ourselves as present to it. And God, says Archbishop Rowan Williams, is "the 'presence' to which all reality is present."[1]

We want to be assured that the mystery is, at heart, benign: a living, loving presence. A great scientific thinker is reported to have remarked, "There is only one important question: Is the universe friendly?"[2]

We are reaching for meanings, asking questions that derive from matters of "ultimate concern." What is the world *for*? What does it mean to be human? Why is our love gifted with such joy, and racked with such pain? Why do certain causes matter so much? Why is existence shadowed always with the threat of failure and loss, and with sometimes unfathomable human evil?

We find ourselves wanting to believe that a living God present to "all that is, seen and unseen"—as the old creed has it—can underwrite with true significance all the delights and tremors, the affirmations and negations, the boring routine and passionate engagement of which human existence is compounded.

We are in need also of power—or, more accurately, empowering. We want to be assured that this wise, loving source of ultimate meaning can *do* something for us, and with us, in times of profoundest need. In the simple old language of Bible and church, we want God to "save" us.

In all these questionings and all this longing Jesus Christ is, for

Christians, the key. Jesus is "God with us," says the birth story in Matthew. "In Christ," declares the Apostle Paul, "God was reconciling the world to himself."[3]

And so this chapter begins an attempt to carry on one side of a kind of conversation about beliefs concerning that divine presence and about our ways of holding those beliefs. Believers need to ask: "What is this God like that I supposedly believe in?" And, strange as this may seem, non-believers need to ask: "What is this "God" like that I (supposedly) *don't* believe in?"

And all need to realize that the best answer to such questions is neither the dogmatic "yes" of the "true believer" nor the atheist's emphatic "no," but the careful"yes *and* no" that is capable of issuing also in a heartfelt "And I *don't* mean maybe!"

Questions to be taken up in this chapter, then, include the following:

- Are there "signs"? Can ordinary experience be referred to that "presence to which all reality is present"?
- Can such signs provide certainty with regard to belief in God?
- Can we, in fact, *fully* know God? If not, how can we know God at all?
- What part can the Bible play in enabling us to know God?
- If questions of *belief about* God have to be answered "yes *and* no," what would it mean for us to say "yes and I *don't* mean maybe!" to the question of *faith in* God?
- What life stance might serve to make us more fully present to that divine presence?

Are there "signs" of divine presence?

'If we assume that the answer to the question "Can we know God?" is "yes," there should be *signs* of that inexpressible mystery. Things in our experience—times of joy or grief, fullness or need, guilty conscience or sense of acceptance, or whatever else—should at least whisper that God is there, available, ready to speak and to listen.[4]

Where should we look? Anywhere and everywhere. But four directions will be identified here. All of us exist in relation to other persons. Persons and personal relationships could offer such a sign. Each of us carries a sense of our unique identity and destiny. The signs may be "within." All of us live within a flow of history which encompasses what we would call our "society" and our "culture." Society and culture may also yield such signs. For all of us there is a physical environment we are in the habit of calling "nature." Nature has always been thought to yield signs of divine presence.

"Nature" a "Sign"?

For many, nature is the first place to look for signals of divine presence. At certain moments, in certain places, many have felt the force of the poet Gerard Manley Hopkins' exclamation: "The world is charged with the grandeur of God!" and of the sentence in Psalm 19 that underlies his words:

> The heavens are telling the glory of God;
> and the firmament proclaims his handiwork.

One such experience as sign given to me stands out in my memory.

> One morning, during a summer vacation in Vermont some years ago, my little daughter and I were walking down the drive from the old farm house we had rented for a few weeks, the trees still dripping from a shower that had just ended.
>
> We happened to look into the woods at the precise moment when a shaft of sunlight made its way far down through the evergreens and showed us a delicate, glistening image, seemingly wheel-shaped. For a moment I could not identify the image. Then I knew: it was a spider's web.
>
> But spider webs are not wheel-shaped. It was a web in the process of being spun; there was the spider, moving steadily, round and round, toward the center. I felt an irrational delight, said "oh" and "ah," and prepared to walk on.
>
> But then I saw (we saw) another similar shape a few feet lower than the first one: another web, another work-in-progress, another spider moving round and round, in the same direction, toward the center.
>
> Now, that must be all, I thought, and once again turned to continue our walk. But my eye caught the same image yet another time, this time a few feet to the left of the other webs: yes, a third web, at the same stage, and a third spider, moving round and round toward the center.
>
> And now we did continue on down the road, and it occurred to me that I had just witnessed something—a coming together of things—that I would in all probability never again be privileged to see.

What happened that morning did not "prove" anything.[5] It was, rather, one of those moments in which something seems to be making itself present to us. If this is sensed as a reality beyond the realities confronting us—whether sea and stars, or mountains and meadows, or perfectly coordinated bodily motion, or spiders creating webs—it may seem to signal what believers speak of as God.

In which case, the wonder and delight inspired in us may arise not just from *our* feelings; they could derive—we imagine at such times—from our participation in an infinitely creative, infinitely receptive yearning and joy. We are assured of this, in fact, in the first Creation story in the Bible (Genesis, chapter l), where we read that God the creator, surveying each new component of that emerging order, "saw that it was good."

Other Persons as "Signs"?

Closer to us than our environing earth are our fellow earth-dwellers and fellow citizens. For those open to the possibility of belief in God, giving attention to what happens in the "between" of human interchange can yield further possible signs of divine presence.

Loving, compassionate actions of others toward *us* can constitute such a sign. To know ourselves loved—what an overwhelming experience it can be!—to sense ourselves as appreciated, as accepted, despite the habitual behaviors we find so *unacceptable* within ourselves. For many, such experiences speak of the presence of one who—simply, straightforwardly (in the words of the First Letter of John)—"*is* love."[6]

It is love also that impels us to a concern for the welfare of those "others" we find sharing our world—especially when we see them suffering injustice and oppression. The Roman Catholic theologian Edward Schillebeeckx argues that one hint of divine presence can be discerned in certain negative reactions we have toward the world as we find it—a shared "no" to the evil, hatred, and misuse of power seen everywhere we turn—along with another disclosure which has the right to our affirming "yes": to the world as, in our best moments, we envision it. In that inner movement—into our "no" and beyond it to our "yes"—we enter into *God's* "no" (divine judgment on our inhumanity) and God's "yes" (divine yearning to bring all to fullness of being). "Something of a sigh of mercy, of compassion," he concludes, "is hidden in the deepest depths of reality, . . . and in it believers hear the name of God."[7]

And what of those special people whom all admire and whom the tradition of the church comes to call "saints," those whose courageous love illumines the darkness of their times? There is Archbishop Desmond Tutu, who time and again denounced and defied the racist system of apartheid in South Africa but was also capable of wading into an angry black crowd to rescue a youth under attack as a supposed traitor to the anti-apartheid cause and who, as chairperson of the Truth and Reconciliation Commission, helped guide his beloved country along the way of acceptance and healing. Or Ruby Bridges, the six-year-old African-American who walked past heckling, even menacing mobs day after day to attend her newly-integrated New Orleans elementary school, praying, in an echo of the words of Jesus from the cross (as remembered in some texts of Luke chapter 23): "Please, dear God, forgive those people, because they don't know what they're doing."[8]

"Signs" in Society and Culture?

We also inhabit a *humanly* created environment. In one of its dimensions it can be called "society"; in another, "culture." That is to say, we are part of a history, which we experience as members of a society and participants in a culture. Given the history of our particular culture, we should not be surprised to encounter, in areas influenced by European presence, many things taken to be, in the context of belief, signs of the holy, loving, active presence of God.

Phrases in our everyday language, for example, like "prodigal son," "Good Samaritan," Promised Land." Similar sayings and images in the language of serious literature and film. Artefacts of our cultural history, viewed by tourists in old New England churches or European cathedrals and abbeys or in art museums everywhere. Echoes heard by concertgoers and CD-listeners, in sublime music drawn from the Bible or the church's liturgy as well as in certain hymns and spirituals and gospel music that continue to be popular, even among nonchurchgoing people.

What does all this add up to? Signs of divine presence as mediated through our social and cultural history? Perhaps. Signs, at least, though, that belief in God *has been* significant, supremely significant, in the history of our American civilization and its European sources, and continues to be an inescapable source of meaning for great numbers of people as this new century and new millennium begin to unfold.

"Signs" Within?

As beings who feel the world "happening" to us and who act on the world "around" us, we also find ourselves *reflecting on* what is taking place. If God can be known by us, then, and if, in the words of Proverbs, "the human spirit is the lamp of the Lord, / searching every innermost part,"[9] there will be elements in that inner experience that could be read as signs of a divine reality. And so our conversation about God, and with God, would be going on within each of us as well as among all of us.

Various reflective people have taken as "signs" of God's presence "within"—and of God's upholding and saving power at work—intimations or insights such as these:

> We are not alone, but divinely companioned: God walks with us, and we with God. This is why, from time to time, our very being may tremble with a sense of awe. Like the patriarch Jacob, after the dream at Bethel, we want to say, "Surely the Lord is in this place—and I did not know it![10]
>
> Our individual existence does not come down to "one damn thing after another" but entails a vocation, a calling to become an authentic person and make a difference in how the world's story comes out. It is not just Moses, at the base of Mount Horeb, or Mary of Nazareth visited by the angel, or Martin Luther King, Jr., sitting in his kitchen in Montgomery, Alabama, who hears such a call, but each of us, no matter what our situation in life.
>
> We do not exist in a context of total randomness, but in a realm which is "ordered"—or, at least, knows "orderings." In his book *Rumor of Angels*, the sociologist Peter Berger suggested that one "sign" of the possible presence of the divine in our world could be the simple ordering gesture of a mother, summoned by an infant crying in the night, who goes to the child, takes the child in her arms (lighting a lamp, perhaps, at the same time), and sits with her, saying, over and over: "Don't be afraid—everything is all right." Her reassuring words to the infant imply a statement with regard to reality as such, an implicit affirmation that there is order in the world, that we can have trust in being.[11]
>
> We are not condemned to unassuageable guilt over our own shortcomings and wrongdoings, but can know ourselves as accepted despite our unworthiness and forgiven for all that plagues our conscience. Nor need

we be forever enslaved by something (an addiction, a structure of character defences) that has seized on us and become a superimposed self, but can find ourselves—as many Twelve Step believers in their "Higher Power" can bear witness—free once again.

We need not wander through life as if in an uncharted wilderness and without a guide, but can avail ourselves of the riches of divine wisdom. A very personal statement of such an assurance appears in an entry in the journal kept by Dag Hammarskjøld, the famous Secretary General of the United Nations: "I don't know," he writes:

> Who—or what—put the question. I don't know when it was put. I don't even remember answering. But at some moment I did answer *Yes* to Someone—or Something—and from that hour I was certain that existence is meaningful and that, therefore, my life, in self-surrender, had a goal.[12]

My dying—and any one of the little dyings along the way—is not a mere falling off into emptiness. The Apostle Paul reminds us that "if we live, we live unto the Lord, and if we die, we die unto the Lord," which means that "whether we live, therefore, or die, we are the Lord's."[13]

Is a "No" to such signs of presence also possible?

These are not self-evident signs. Each could be read as if its alleged significance is a mere projection of our human need—for companionship and understanding, for merciful acceptance in the face of sensed wrongdoings, for meaning in the endeavors we undertake, for something in life our death cannot obliterate.

God as present to, and in, nature? Many would endorse the response made by the eighteenth-century French astronomer and mathematician Pierre Simon LaPlace to a question about God as creator: "I have no need of that hypothesis." Or the declaration of the late Carl Sagan, in his introduction to Stephen Hawking's best-selling *A Brief History of Time*, that for Hawking and for other researchers and theorists like him, their findings suggest no "edge" to the universe, no beginning or end in time, and "nothing for a Creator to do."[14]

As for signs of divine presence in human relationships of love and compassion: unbelievers would question this form of "that hypothesis" also—the belief that God constitutes the "between" in our relationships of love and friendship, accounting for the ties that bind to family and friends, the desire to help others in need, or that mixture of need and affinity most often pointed to by the word "love."

Rock singer John Lennon may have voiced the creed, years ago, that many non-religious people subscribe to, whether they realize it or not. In a song listing his several "don't believes," he ends with the only affirmation he finds himself able to make about personal being and relationship: "I just believe in me, Yoko and me—that's reality."[15]

Elements of Western society and culture as signs of divine presence and activity? It is here, probably, that nonbelief can bring out its heaviest weaponry. Secularist participants in our life together would agree that this society is "God-haunted." But they would point out that this is a very mixed, even contradictory, heritage. We cannot suppress cultural memories of Christian societies responsible for such atrocities as the hunting down of women accused of being "witches"; the hounding of seekers after scientific and philosophical truth—the 17th-century astronomer Galileo being merely the most famous of these; and, all too recently, the never to be forgotten degradation and mass slaughter—in those "believing" nations called Germany, Poland, Italy, and France where huge numbers of "Christians" stood by saying and doing nothing—of millions whose crime consisted in being Jews, or gypsies, or homosexuals.

The suggestion that there are signs "within"—that human beings are creatures made "in the image of God" to walk with God, to exist in relationship with God—comes under fierce attack as well. Such a claim will be written off by many as "wish-fulfillment fantasy," futile attempts to evade the fully-secular realization, hinted at in the last faltering interchange of Edward Albee's *Who's Afraid of Virginia Woolf,* that all there is in the world is "just us."[16]

Can we say *both* "yes" *and* "no" to the question of divine presence?

Saying "no" to the question "Can we know God?" is something we can choose to do, in unbelief. But, importantly, it is also something we *must* do, as believers. That's because any "yes" answer we can give to this question has to include a "no," has to be, in fact, a "yes *and* no."

What does such a negation point to? To begin with, it points to that in God which we cannot know, to an unknowable element that has to be there if the name "God" is to have any meaning or use for us.

This "no" must be an indicator of authentic mystery, however, not an instrument for phony mystification. A student of mine who happened to be a minister's son complained once, in a class discussion, that whenever he asked a hard question about religion his father the man of God would say, "It's a mystery of faith, son, a mystery of faith." Such evasion does not do honor to the divine mystery and the wrestling required of all who would engage the angel of that mystery. Religion, Peter Gomes has said, "is not an escape from reality but rather a genuine effort to make sense of what passes for reality."[17]

The sense of such mystery can suggest that there is a "beyondness," a "more," in reality itself, that it is this which provides the ground for and the lure of creative possibility, that we are in truth unceasingly offered possibilities for newness by the One who is the source and fulfillment of all that is.

In which case, the fullness of that which offers these possibilities could never be "known" by us. It would have to be infinitely beyond our knowing, this Reality that grounds and guides and gathers in all the separate-but-related realities of our individual existence, our relationships with other human beings, our involvement in the history of a particular society and culture and of the whole human family, and our participation in the unimaginably complex being of this planet, this galaxy, and the cosmos of which that galaxy is only a minute component.

Can we know God? No, says Job, at the end of the long shouting match and after the deliverances of the voice from the whirlwind: "I have uttered what I did not understand, things too wonderful for me, which I did not know." No, says the Apostle Paul: "O the depths of the riches and wisdom and knowledge of God! How unsearchable are his judgments and how inscrutable his ways"! No, says the author of the First Letter to Timothy, for "it is [God] alone who has immortality and dwells in unapproachable light, whom no one has ever seen or can see."[18]

Is ultimate reality both veiled and revealed—and "re-veiled"?

This "no" to the question "Can we know God?" is, however, a qualified "no." For God is an "unknown" whom we, somehow, also "know." In terms (again) of relationship—I know a person whom I love and who loves me only in so far as that person makes herself, or himself, known. Even this will be a limited knowing; impenetrable mystery will remain. But, as anyone who has loved and been loved can attest, such knowing can be profoundly fulfilling, with all its limitations and frustrations.

And the element of *un*knowing can become, in a strange way, part of the knowing—a sign of the mystery that is at the center of the one known and of the knower and in the "between" of the relationship itself; a sign, as well, of the "more" always available in the future of that relationship.

All would depend, then, on God's initiative. The presence of God is a *veiled* presence: "Truly," we read in Isaiah, "truly you are a God who hides himself, / O God of Israel, the Savior." But it can be at the same time a *revealed* presence. For this same "high and lofty one who inhabits eternity," we are told a few chapters later, dwells "with those who are contrite and humble in spirit."[19]

The Apostle Paul develops this idea further. "What human being knows what is truly human," he asks, "except the human spirit that is within? So also no one comprehends what is truly God's except the Spirit of God." And where does this leave us? Paul insists that we, as people of faith, "have received not the spirit of the world, but the Spirit that is from God." To what end? "So that we may understand the gifts bestowed on us by God."[20]

In God's exercise of the divine freedom—just as in our human freedom—something of the divine reality is revealed and something (necessarily) remains inaccessible. For God is "Other," we say; the divine reality is "beyond"—beyond our comprehension, surpassing our supremest visions and our most exalted endeavors.

At the same time, it is vital to insist that this God who must be known as beyond is never to be imagined as a *distant* God, unapproachable by us. No, God is—as the twentieth century German theologian and martyr Dietrich Bonhoeffer wrote—the "beyond *in the midst*."[21] The veiling and the revealing are both happening, for all of us, here, now. In every slightest turn in the story any one of us is living, an aura can be glimpsed, an overtone half heard, that is *God's* story making itself known as an offer of possibility whereby our story can find, right there, right then, its center of meaning, its ground of security, its warrant for action, and its fulfillment in eternal peace.

Again, this beyondness of God must not be read in terms of coercive *power*, either, so that we envision the divine presence simply as overwhelming our human intellect and will. God does not violate anyone's freedom, any more than we can override what we might understand as God's freedom. We cannot "have" God. At the same time, the relationship is such that God does not "have" us either. God's intention comes to us as invitation; God's power is felt not as coercion but persuasion.

The divine reality is veiled for another reason as well: *sinfulness*, the distorted perceptions and destructive dispositions of our "fallen" humanity. Not only unable to grasp the whole truth, we are often also unwilling to act according to the truth we know.

Instead of responding to the possibilities in a situation with the trust and creativity available to us, we react with fear, or aggressiveness and bravado. We close off risky creative directions and, instead, "play it safe." Despairing of ever breaking free from our addictive behavior, we become more and more compulsive. We drown out the serious questioner inside with the noise of sitcoms, small talk, or our own unceasing mental chatter. We nurse wounds suffered by our self-esteem, allowing ourselves to become more and more self-absorbed or, in those connections we do manage to sustain, more and more domineering or manipulative.

Or—falling into what the Bible means by "idolatry"—we redirect the passion at the center of our being toward something unworthy of what, with God, we could become. We seek to assuage that divine discontent, to realize that dimly glimpsed vision, by way of a personal attachment, a system of belief, a pastime, or even an unassailable security, to which we (as it were) pray: "Be everything to me!" or complain: "Why can't you be everything to me?"

Can we know God as self-revealed, in Holy Scripture?

The discussion so far has involved some "cheating." It *could* be argued that God can be known simply from signs such as nature, human relationship, cultural history, and inner promptings. At the beginning of his Letter to the Romans, the Apostle Paul suggests that this knowing is available to everyone. It should be "plain to them," he says, "because God has shown it to them . . . through the things he has made."[22]

Actually, however, none of us receives clues about God by way of such "innocent," first-ever experience. As already made clear, we live in a culture steeped in the traditions, and pervaded by the images and symbols, deriving from the Christian religion and from what it has made of its Judaic origins. Our ways of looking at the natural world, or evaluating relationships, or understanding human existence are likely to be, in large part, already formed according to Judaic-Christian influences. According to what is found—to be even more direct about it—in the Bible.

For Christianity, along with the other religions—Judaism and Islam—claiming to derive from ancient Abraham, affirms that the divine reality has been revealed to humankind. Those seeking to walk through human existence as pilgrims of faith need not merely reflect on their lives *as if* there were a God; they can come to affirm God *as* everything required for the fulfillment of those lives in wonder, creativity, self-worth, courage, the "glorious exchanges" of life in community, responsible service to fellow earth-dwellers, and "peace at the last."

For these "people of the Book," Scripture comes to the forefront—the writings held by such believers to be "sacred." In them, they declare, their God is self-revealed. In them the ultimate meanings of those realities earlier identified as signs are illumined—not just illumined *by* us, through our own imaginative insights, but, through God's gracious initiative, somehow also illumined *for* us.

Since Christians claim to know God as uniquely present to the world in the man called Jesus of Nazareth, their statements of belief will focus particularly on the witness of the New Testament[23] and present Jesus likewise in relation to the signs and their meaning. For Christians find in Jesus as the Christ the heart of what God is revealed to be in those earlier writings called the Old Testament: the ground of our hope for eternal life, our reconciler and liberator, our covenant partner, and, in the mystery of the God who is both three and one, our creator and provider.

If faith is (in the words of Alan Jones) "the willingness to have one's story tested by a larger narrative that one takes on trust,"[24] what is there in that biblical "larger narrative" that can address both what we find ourselves affirming as to the ecstasies and settled joys life can bring and what we find ourselves afflicted with by way of anxiety, loneliness, self-absorption, prejudice, hatred and violence, and the threat of an ultimate sense of meaninglessness as we make our way toward the "undiscovered country" of death?

A Preliminary Look at that "Larger Story" Found in Holy Scripture

What kinds of things are found between the covers of the Christian Bible, what difficulties this collection of writings presents, and how it can best be read by those who seek to know the God to which it gives witness—these are topics for a later chapter: "Is the Bible the 'Word of God'?" The attempt now—overleaping those questions and problems for the moment—will be to offer a rough version of a biblical depiction of God as discerned by way of the approach to Scripture to be advocated here.

This is a *living* God, the Bible seems to tell us, one who experiences "godfully" what we undergo humanly: feelings, visions of possibility, purposes frustrated and purposes fulfilled; one who makes a difference in the world, who (we dare to say) "acts." It is not that we humans simply manage to discern a pattern of meaning in life and the world and then decide to live out that meaning as best we may. This is not a humanism.

No, what we have to do with—all Scripture insists—is "the living God," whom we know and by whom we are known. God and we are in *relationship*. And this relationship is characterized—as all true relationship must be—by interchange in freedom. God is free to be God, with all that this entails as to the patient, persuasive working of divine love, justice, creativity, and wisdom in all things. And humans—by virtue of being "in God's image"—are free to be human. A later chapter will develop the idea that there is even something like freedom in what has traditionally been called "nature."

According to the view of God informing this discussion,[25] it is of the very nature of God not to override these other freedoms. The story of humankind, then, read in biblical terms—centering on the New Testament's witness to that representative human being Jesus of Nazareth—has to do primarily (in the words of the poet T. S. Eliot) with "the drawing of this Love and the voice of this Calling"[26]: God's offer of abiding love exercised according to infinite wisdom within a matrix of eternal life.

Such a relational model permits us to envision God as, so to speak, the infinite improviser. This musicianly God eternally holds in mind all the potentialities of rhythm, melody, tone quality, harmony, and compositional form—all the capabilities, in other words, of this instrument called being. God remembers at any moment in time's flow all the themes so far advanced and all the variations so far undertaken. And God always evokes the most satisfying sounds possible with what the moment makes available.

There is an aspect of God, in other words, in which ineffable music remains eternally possible, and in some sense eternally realized. There is another aspect in which the music of the world's history—its hard-won harmonies and unbearable cacophonies—is also sounding and somehow, at the same time, being integrated into the celestial performance whose participants include "every creature in heaven and on earth and under the earth and in the sea."[27]

The question—Can we know God?—has shifted its meaning now. And so have the possible "yes" and "no" answers. For what has been implied here is that we cannot help "knowing" God, in the sense of existing in relationship with God. The revised question, then, would concern the *quality* of that relationship, according to how we respond, in freedom, to the opportunities made available.

"Do you know Jack?" I am asked. "Yes," I reply. And then, after a second, "Yes, but—." Which is to say, yes, I have made Jack's acquaintance, but am now aware of so much more to be known that it is as if we remain relative strangers. Or I respond: "No," and then, "No, but—." My first sense is of not knowing Jack, but I soon realize I *am* aware of this person, while at the same time having to admit that's as far as my knowledge goes. Still another response is possible, as well, something more like a yes-*and*-no answer. Yes, I am acquainted with Jack, and more than casually so; but at the same time, no, the depths of possibility in the relationship are such that it's almost as if I do not know the person in question. However, I very much want the acquaintance to deepen, and will do my part to make this happen.

Reading Holy Scripture in this relational way, then, we can know God as creator and provider, and at the same time know Jesus Christ to be the one in whom "all things in heaven and on earth were created."[28] And we can do this without limiting ourselves to an uncritical acceptance of the prescientific image of God as "maker" of all that is or a desperate clinging to the image of God as "magician," manipulating anything and everything in our behalf.

We can also experience God, in this way—in and with Jesus Christ, understood to be "Emmanuel": "God with us"—as covenant partner, with new understandings of ancient images for that relationship like those of king, or father, or judge. In the stories about this God and the "people of the covenant" we can squirm with human negotiators trying to adjust the terms so as to get what seems the "better deal" or exult, and suffer, with them in their courageous though all-too-human efforts to take hold of God's risky better way. And we can share, imaginatively, the frustrations and small triumphs of a God who chooses to walk with us, both in our babiest steps and our greatest strides.

As for the many occasions when our sinfulness thwarts the divine creative intent and disrupts the covenant relationship, God can be known by us then as liberator and reconciler, or—in the traditional language—as "savior." The face of God thus revealed is that of the wronged parent of the "prodigal son" (Luke chapter 15), catching sight of the returning son "while he was still far off" and running—"filled with compassion"—to "put his arms around [the son] and kiss him." And of the healer who, the Gospels tell us, acted again and again, in behalf of God, to free persons enfettered by powers beyond their strength, "possessed" (in the thought-forms of the time) by "demons."

Finally, a God can be set forth who is for us the source and hope of eternal life. The Bible is honeycombed with promises about a being with God, or in God, that is not limited to the lifetime of an individual or a people or an institution or a civilization, but is indeed—as in certain sayings attributed to Jesus—"eternal life."

The point of such talk is not to provide information about "life after death," and "heaven," and other "last things." It is, rather, as with all the teachings of Holy Scripture, to evoke truths concerning the relationship between God and us. For the reasoning behind all the imagery and speculations concerning heaven is this: We are in God. God is characterized as having eternal life. Therefore we also, in God, have eternal life.[29] That is to say, the presence of God does not, at our death, turn into an absence: our walk with God goes on. Or, as Paul puts it—in that strong, simple statement from Romans chapter 14 already quoted—"If we live, we live to the Lord, and if we die, we die to the Lord; so then, whether we live or whether we die, we are the Lord's."[30]

Can we say "yes *and* no" to questions of belief and say "I *don't* mean maybe!" to God?

The question is this: Can we learn to live with the tension, to say "yes *and* no" to the indispensable but always problematic formulations of belief and, at the same time, "I *don't* mean maybe" to the God with whom we are in living relationship? Can we remain resolved to walk with God, to follow out all the potential signs in the direction of "beyond" so that the divine presence will thus be enabled to disclose itself to us? Can we learn to live with changing answers and with new elements in the relationship? Is it possible for us who seek both faith and belief to be broadminded, tolerant, aware of both sides on an issue, and still have convictions, make hard choices, live for something, even be ready to die for something?

Or—"Maybe," After All?

"Maybe" is the response great numbers of people want to make on this issue. For some, the lack of firm, "factual" evidence either way on issues of belief makes the "slantwise nod" seem the appropriate response.

Others simply surrender to the spirit of "maybe" that has become part of the air we breathe. Some of these are people whose "yeses" that are actually "maybes" inflate the positive figures in polls asking about belief in God. They may be occasional church attenders. Many are *non*-attenders: "home Baptists" (as the joking expression has it), or lapsed but still attached Catholics—and those numerous others who claim to find God best in the woods or the garden.

And what about that powerful alternative offer: modern secularist consumerism and "recreationism"? As "secular" beings, we can get along perfectly well without reference to anything that might be *beyond* the resources of this world. And, many would add, we can then focus on material or physical realities rather than on "spiritual" realities—or, as we say these days, "values." The slogan for such an existence?—not "be all you can be" so much as "buy all you can buy."

Frequently, the "maybe" answer derives from unhappy encounters with religion itself—with the church or with church people. Some claim to have tried religion and found it wanting. At times, such a response may be simply an effect of expectations, fostered by the entertainment culture already spoken of, for instant "payoff." "I went to church a couple of times," a person will say, "but it didn't do anything for me." As if religious observance should yield its benefits right now, the way a sitcom will throw a laugh line at us within seconds of its opening or a lottery ticket tell us, as soon as we scratch it, whether we have or have not won something.

But such disappointment is, often enough, justified. Perhaps, during a church-going time in one's life, supposedly "holy" people turned out to be indifferent, or mean-spirited. Perhaps a pastor was simply not "there" when the heartbreak was happening. Perhaps someone needing a church open to questioning, a safe place for uncertainty and doubt, found instead an atmosphere that was suffocatingly closed-minded and judgmental. If that's the best the self-proclaimed representatives of the faith can do—and we still can't quite manage a no to religion more generally—why not just say "maybe"?

And yet—the answer cannot be "maybe." Too much is at stake here for a shrugging dismissal of the question of belief. In the very nature of the case, to believe in God is to entrust one's life. The "great commandment" calls on us to "love the Lord [our] God with all [our] heart, and with all [our] soul, and with all [our] mind."[31] To believe in God is to place our stories, as was suggested earlier, into a "larger story" taken on trust.

To all that has been set forth—the signs of divine presence in the world and the witness to God's dealings with humankind found in Holy Scripture—a response of "maybe" is manifestly insufficient. Taking such a position is like standing before a minister or rabbi, or a justice of the peace, for that matter, having just heard the question meaning: "Will you have this man/woman to be your life partner?" and delivering the answer: "Maybe." For all that has been described here centers in relationship. In answering "yes," or "I will," in such a ceremony, one is not affirming "I know everything there is to know about this other person, and about myself, and about the possibilities in this union." Nor is one declaring that there will never be any difficulties in future years, any doubts of one another, any occasions requiring apologies and renewed effort. What the "yes" or "I will" is saying is something like this: We have been together long enough, have talked and worked and played together sufficiently, have checked out the signs with enough care, that I feel ready to make this commitment to a life together and to all that this might demand of me.

It is in this sense—and in this context of a relationship grounded in a kind of knowing but requiring trust and commitment rather than unquestioning certitude—that the answer to the question "Can we know God?" turns out to be not "maybe" but "yes." Not a resounding yes, necessarily, incorporating clear definitions of that to which assent is thus being given, but something more like the "yes-*and*-no" cry of the man asking Jesus to heal his chronically ill son: "Lord, I believe; help my unbelief!"[32]

Toward a Life Practice that Says "I Don't Mean Maybe"

One way of understanding an existence lived in such a spirit of "I don't mean maybe" is presented by anthropologist and social philosopher Ernest Becker, in his Pulitzer Prize-winning book, *The Denial of Death*.[33] Becker's theme, over all, is the problem of heroism. Each of us, he maintains, wants to be a hero, or—better, perhaps—each of us wants to perform heroically the life task given us. But what is it that can impart the heroism the life task demands?

Not our own self-valuing, Becker insists. Nor publicly recognized achievements, Not even other persons—whether hero figures with whom we try to identify ourselves or objects of our romantic (and sexual) desire in whom we seek to lose ourselves. We cannot ask a human being to be "a god-like 'everything' to another." For "no human relationship can bear the burden of godhood."[34]

Even our most strenuous efforts at self-understanding cannot suffice. As Becker writes elsewhere in the same chapter, "All the analysis in the world doesn't allow . . . persons to find out *who they are* and why they are here on earth, why they have to die, and how they can make their life a triumph."[35]

What *can* enable us to achieve a heroic performance of our life's task, Becker declares, is the "creative solution." This strategy for soul-making demands, first, that we see the elements of our life situation, including our sense of life as assignment or calling, as components of one great, complex problem. (That part we don't find very hard to do!) Next, we are asked to turn that problem, the problem constituted by any human existence, into a creative work, the way an artist does. And then, finally, we are encouraged to offer that work of art, as a gift, to its projected audience.

"Audience"? What audience? The only appropriate, and adequate, audience—Becker concludes—for the life-as-art offerings of all of us, the most obscure among us as well as the most celebrated and famous, is God, "the presence [once again] to which all reality is present." Not oneself, not the loved other, not the (now-adoring, now-indifferent) public—but God. "The artist's gift is always to creation itself, to the ultimate meaning of life, to God."[36]

What is extended at this point, therefore, is an urgent invitation to say "yes," not "maybe," to our own existence, to the possibility of divine presence in us and our world, and to the possibility of a vital relationship with the God thus present. To the possibility, as well—given this book's focus on Christianity—that the man Jesus of Nazareth, identified and believed in as "God with us," offers both a unique manifestation of that divine reality and an incomparable way of living out that relationship.

This is also a challenge to say "yes," not "maybe," to some of the endeavors, the disciplines, the spiritual practices whereby an individual existence can become, under God, a heroically creative venture. Take your life up—seriously, humorously—as a "problem." Using whatever comes to hand, compose from those problematic materials—including the beliefs to which you are learning to say "yes *and* no"—an existence which is your work of art and, at the same time, part of God's artistic endeavor in the world. And lift it up, in joy and anguish, praise and petition—every day as well as on the last day—to the One from whom comes its initiating impulse and its lifelong sustaining power and by whom it is ultimately received with infinite appreciation and unending love.

ENDNOTES

[1] Rowan Williams, *Resurrection: Interpreting the Easter Gospel* (Harrisburg, PA,: Morehouse Publishing, 1994), 29.

[2] Attributed, by some, to Albert Einstein. Huston Smith, on the other hand, cites the nineteenth-century zoologist Ernst Haeckel, in *Why Religion Matters: The Fate of the Human Spirit in an Age of Disbelief* (HarperSanFrancisco, 2001), 26.

[3] 2 Corinthians 5:19.

[4] In *The House of Wisdom*, a sustained theological meditation carried on during a year of "pilgrimage," John S. Dunne identifies four such insights into divine presence: "Things are meant." "There are signs." "The heart speaks." "There is a way." *The House of Wisdom: A Pilgrimage* (San Francisco: Harper and Row, 1985).

[5] Some Christian thinkers have attempted to set out arguments, or "proofs," that might demonstrate the existence of God—arguing, for example, from the evidence of design in the universe to an originating intelligence. To many modern philosophers and theologians, however, such arguments do not so much "prove" that there is a God as lend a kind of secondary support to a belief in God adhered to on other grounds.

[6] 1 John 4:16. Longsuffering love toward others must not be confused, however, with the acceptance of exploitation and abuse. A person with an abusive partner or parent, while showing divine love in seeking to understand that person and desiring the best for that person's life, should also demonstrate divine justice by getting out of the situation in which abuse is regularly perpetrated or insisting on appropriate changes in the abuser's behavior.

[7] Edward Schillebeeckx, *Church: The Human Story of God* (New York: Crossroad, 1993), 5-6.

[8] Robert Coles, *Harvard Diary: Reflections on the Sacred and the Secular* (New York: Crossroad, 1988), 113-14, 143.

[9] Proverbs 20:27.

[10] Genesis 28:16.

[11] Peter L. Berger, *A Rumor of Angels: Modern Society and the Rediscovery of the Supernatural* (Garden City, N.Y.: Doubleday, 1970), 54-55.

[12] Dag Hammarskjøld, *Markings*, trans. Leif Sjøberg and W. H. Auden (New York: Ballantine Books, 1983), 180.

[13] Romans 14:7-8.

[14] Stephen Hawking, *A Brief History of Time: From the Big Bang to Black Holes* (Toronto: Bantam Books, 1988), x.

[15] John Lennon, "God" (Nashville: Sony—ATV Music Publishing).

[16] Edward Albee, *Who's Afraid of Virginia Woolf?* (New York: Pocket Books, 1963; originally published by Athenaeum House, 1962). A recent book addressing the prevalence of a secular worldview is Huston Smith's*Why Religion Matters: The Fate of the Human Spirit in an Age of Disbelief* (HarperSanFrancisco, 2001)

[17] Peter J. Gomes, *The Good Book: Reading the Bible with Mind and Heart* (New York: William Morrow, 1996), 213.

[18] Job 42:3; Romans 11:33; 1 Timothy 6:16.

[19] Isaiah 45:15; 57:15.

[20] 1 Corinthians 2:11-12

[21] Cited in Marilynne Robinson, *The Death of Adam: Essays on Modern Thought* (Boston: Houghton Mifflin, 1998), 124.

[22] Romans 1:19-20.

[23] The traditional labels "New Testament" and "Old Testament" can give a false impression of relative status for these two parts of the Christian Bible, suggesting that the one has superseded, even invalidated, the other. On the other hand, alternatives such as "Hebrew Scripture" (over against "New Testament"), or "older" and "newer" testaments (the usage of Canadian theologian Douglas John Hall) present their own problems. In this book, therefore, the traditional language will be adhered to—reluctantly, and without suggesting that the value of the Old Testament depends intrinsically on its being "fulfilled" by the New.

[24] Alan Jones, *The Soul's Journey: Exploring the Three Passages of the Spiritual Life with Dante as a Guide* (HarperSanFrancisco, 1995), 199.

[25] The line of thinking found here and elsewhere in the book owes much to what is known in theological circles as "Process" thought—an understanding of God and the world, influenced strongly by philosopher Alfred North Whitehead and theologian Charles Hartshorne, which emphasizes event, becoming, and relatedness rather than (as in many earlier theologies) substance and being.

Introductions to the Process approach to Christian believing can be found in John

B. Cobb, Jr., and David Ray Griffin, *Process Theology: An Introductory Exposition* (Philadelphia: Westminster Press, 1976); Marjorie Hewitt Suchocki, *God—Christ—Church: A Practical Guide to Process Theology*, rev. ed. (New York: Crossroad, 1989); and Burton Z. Cooper,*Why, God?* (Atlanta: John Knox Press, 1988), Chapter 4.

[26] T. S. Eliot, "Little Gidding," in *Complete Poems and Plays 1909-1950* (New York: Harcourt, Brace, 1952), 145.

[27] Revelation 5:13.

[28] Colossians 1:16.

[29] This "we" should not be read as restricted to those who call themselves "Christians": See, in Chapter Seven, the section "Is Jesus *the* way to God?"

[30] Romans 14:8

[31] Matthew 22:37-38, quoting Deuteronomy 6:5.

[32] Mark 9:24.

[33] Ernest Becker, *The Denial of Death* (New York: Free Press, 1973).

[34] Becker, *Denial*, 166.

[35] Becker, *Denial*, 193.

[36] Becker, *Denial*, 173.

CHAPTER TWO

Is the Bible the "Word of God"?
A Further Question about God as Self-Revealing Mystery

Christian faith directs us to seek the ultimate meaning of such signs of divine presence as those already identified by turning to the stories, images and sayings of Holy Scripture. It urges us to let our story be "tested" by [this] "larger story." And it finds the central meaning of that larger story in the life and death and rising to new life of Jesus of Nazareth.

Is this Bible, then—as Christians insist—the "Word of God"? Our response, once again, has to encompass both a "yes" and a "no." Something is there of God's self-revealing, to which we must learn to respond in eager obedience. But everything therein revealed is also "veiled." It comes to us as text, as language requiring interpretation. Which is to say, words about happenings involving a particular people at a particular time—presented in the language and thought-forms of that alien people and that long-ago time—must be enabled to speak in very different times and places.

"Veiled" by natural creaturely limitation, this revelation has been "re-veiled" as well, through sinful dispositions. Some things in the Bible are difficult; some are just wrong. Our interpretations of those texts will likewise be both limited by our lack of knowledge and sensitivity and warped by reason of our sinfulness. What was said earlier about the "beyondness," the "hiddenness," of God's own being applies also to God's own book (so to speak), the Bible. What God truly is infinitely surpasses our comprehension; likewise, the mingled truth and distortion in God's self-revealing by way of Holy Scripture endlessly frustrates our efforts at a complete sorting out.

Questions taken up in the sorting out this chapter attempts include the following:

- Are the happenings narrated in the Bible all "true"?
- Are all the moral assumptions of the Bible "right"?

- What is "biblical fundamentalism"? How are fundamentalists different from those they would call "liberals"?
- How is it possible to give a "yes-*and*-no" answer to questions concerning fact and value in the Bible?
- What do we need to do to make a "yes-*and*-no" approach to the Bible work for us?
- What enables us to respond to the biblical writings not only with "yes *and* no" but also with "and I *don't* mean maybe!"?

Before opening these lines of questioning, though, it would be helpful to review what is to be found in the writings—or collection of writings (which is what "Bible" basically means)—under scrutiny here.

The "Larger Story" in the Old and New Testaments

For the earliest Christians, the object of worship continued to be the God self-revealed in relation to a particular people, Israel, in dealings witnessed to by the narratives, prophecy, wisdom writings, and poetry revered by Jews and Christians as "holy scripture."

What was available for them remains available, of course, for those reading the Bible now. There are, first, the well-known stories of beginnings, from Genesis (the "book of beginnings")—cosmic beginnings, human beginnings, and the beginnings of the people Israel.

The next four books—Exodus, Leviticus, Numbers, and Deuteronomy—concern the "exodus" and "wilderness wanderings" of those descendants of the patriarch Jacob (renamed "Israel") who believed themselves to have been rescued from oppression in Egypt, instructed—during their journeying—in the ways of their God Yahweh, and guided toward what was for them the "land of promise."

The "history" writings (Joshua, Judges, the two books of Samuel, and the two books of Kings, along with the Chronicles—covering the 13th through the 7th centuries BCE) present the settlement of that land, the establishment of a monarchy, and the decline of what had become (later) the divided kingdoms of Israel and Judah, eventuating in the virtual wiping out of the Northern Kingdom and the deportation to the far away land of Babylon of the leading figures and families of Judah. The books of Ezra and Nehemiah concern those exiles who returned to Jerusalem and its environs (in the 6th and 5th centuries BCE) to rebuild the city and restore the Temple and its worship.

There are also, very importantly, the prophetic writings—the inspired responses of those strange, impassioned carriers of faith and fallibility we call prophets to the significant events of their times—books like Amos, Isaiah, Hosea, Jeremiah, and others.

Sayings and discourses from the "Wisdom tradition," as well—

some centering on the how-to's of a good and wise existence (Proverbs), others wrestling with the what and why of the human condition (Job, Ecclesiastes). And, finally, varieties of lyric poetry, as in the Psalms and the Song of Solomon, along with a few short-story-like narratives: Ruth, Jonah, and Esther.

But the people of the Jesus movement were coming to read these Scriptures under the conviction that in Jesus of Nazareth this God of Israel was bringing in the new age, the "kingdom of God," foretold in those same writings. Not only did they receive the words and deeds of Jesus as a revelation *from* God; they were increasingly perceiving the *person* of Jesus as a revelation *of* God. Early preachers of the Christian message constantly used the phrase "according to the scriptures"; but whenever they did, it was with reference to something understood as pointing, for its deepest meaning, toward the mission, the death, and the rising again of Jesus.

Out of this process of reinterpretation emerged specifically Christian writings, some of which came to take on scriptural status themselves as the "New Testament."[1] The subject of these writings, too—as with those of the Old Testament—is God self-revealed through happenings in the world reflected on and interpreted by persons involved in the happenings and "inspired" to convey their world-changing meaning.

The persons so involved, in this case, were not prophets, but "apostles" and "evangelists." Apostles proclaimed the "gospel"—the "good news" of what God was doing in Jesus as the Christ—in spoken and, sometimes, written words. The evangelists, in this same context, did their proclaiming by creating those written representations of what Jesus did and who Jesus was—to the eyes and ears of faith—that came to be called gospels.

The first of the writings later to make up this New Testament were the "letters." Most of these were written by a convert from Tarsus named Saul, who as an apostle came to be better known—by his Roman name—as Paul. Others were credited to Paul though not actually written by him, and still others came to be associated, by tradition, with apostolic names like Peter or James or John.

Though the letters, addressed to congregations or groups of churches, tended to take up particular questions troubling those believers, they also conveyed powerful understandings of what it means to believe in Jesus as representing God among humankind. The church came to see these writings as conveying an "inspired" understanding—one influenced, that is, by the promptings of God's Spirit—to be considered as authoritative for the church.

Meanwhile, with the generation of "eyewitnesses" dying out, and with a large and growing variety of stories about Jesus in circulation, a need was felt to provide authorized written accounts of Jesus' words and works, conveying the "good news" of who Jesus essentially was and what had been accomplished through him.

Thus arose the gospels already referred to—four of them: the one attributed to Mark first (probably around the year 70 C.E.); then, some years later, Matthew and Luke, incorporating much of the material from the first gospel but making use of other sources as well; and that odd-one-out among the gospels: John, seemingly a sustained reflection, within a narrative framework, on the meaning of Jesus' person and work.

The same "Luke" responsible, according to tradition, for the third gospel composed a sequel called the "Acts of the Apostles," describing what he understood to be the ongoing work of the risen Jesus through the power of the Holy Spirit under the leadership, especially, of the apostles Peter and Paul. And around the end of the century, a person from one of a group of churches in Asia Minor (Turkey, on todays' maps), living in exile on a tiny island in the Aegean Sea, wrote what many consider the strangest book in the Bible—"The Revelation to John"—famous because of its use of bizarre images and symbols to present scenes supposedly relating happenings of that time to the end of the world and the establishing of the City of God, the New Jerusalem.

Why would anyone say "No" to the Bible as the "Word of God"?

For many centuries in the history of the West, it was almost unthinkable that one might seriously disbelieve the Bible. By both church leaders and ordinary folk the Bible was revered as an obviously holy book. It was simply assumed that, properly interpreted, it would provide its readers with—they would say, more directly: it *was*—the "Word of God."

And great comfort and courage—and life wisdom—their reading of the Bible gave them! For they learned of a creation that the Creator found to be "very good." They invoked the guidance of One who was their "shepherd," leading them "by still waters," walking with them even "through the valley of the shadow of death." They heard words of Jesus blessing the "poor in spirit" and the "peacemakers" and "those who hunger and thirst for righteousness," along with stories about a "prodigal son" and his welcoming father and a despised Samaritan helping a desperate Jew beside the road leading down to Jericho, and last words of caring and forgiveness and promise spoken from the cross—the list (as anyone at all acquainted with the Bible knows well) is very long.

Many in "Christian America," however—and in "post-Christian" Europe—are prepared to answer the question "Is the Bible the 'Word of God'?" with a "no." To what they have found, or heard of, in the Holy Book they respond, with *Porgy and Bess*'s Sportin' Life, "It ain't necessarily so." And some of these out-loud or under-the-breath nay-sayers will be self-professed Christians seeking a revised understanding of the relation between God and the Bible, or trying to ignore the issue—while secretly feeling, perhaps, that the upholders of a literalist approach to the Bible are the *real* believers.

To this sign of divine presence as well, then, critical questions are posed: Can all of what is set forth there be established as *true?* And what about that which so many find to be *not right,* falling short of an adequate understanding of fully-realized humanity?

It Ain't Necessarily "True."

If by true we mean literally, factually true, then much of what is to be found between the covers of this revered book can be judged to be untrue.

Even the *children* of modernity can have the sense, about such matters, that "it ain't necessarily so"—as this fragment of a conversation between my son and me (years ago, when he was seven or eight) suggests.

> Son (from the back seat of the car): Dad, you know those stories in the Bible?
> Father: Yes. What about them?
> Son: Are they real or fake?
> Father (cautiously): Some of them are very real. Why do you ask?
> Son: Well, they sound fake to me.

The Bible is full of stories presenting God's involvement in human history. But, the modern mind may want to ask, are these all true stories? That is to say, did these things really happen that way? Are the facts correct? There are obvious grounds for believing that the answer to such a line of questioning could often be "no." Does the story of the human race begin with two persons in a mideastern garden, one of whom has been assembled from a rib extracted from the other? Is the universal flood spoken of in Genesis chapters 6-9 even remotely a possibility? Did the walls of Jericho fall down flat—archeological evidence completely to the contrary—at the shouts and trumpet blasts of some Hebrew invaders?[2]

As for the Christian writings—do we want to insist that Jesus actually walked on water or called Lazarus, four days gone, from the tomb? In light of the findings of contemporary scholarship—the work of the Jesus Seminar, for example[3]—can we be sure that, if we had been among those following Jesus in first-century Palestine, we would actually have heard Jesus say all the things he is reported to have said or seen Jesus do all the healings and exorcisms he is supposed to have done?

Are such stories and such suppositions "real" or "fake"? In factual terms, a lot of them "sound fake"—and not just to seven- or eight-year-old children!

It Ain't Necessarily "Right."

No one, not even the most ardent anti-religionist, would deny that the Bible can offer words of matchless wisdom. But many even among its most devout readers stumble across images and stories so demeaning of certain elements of our cherished humanity that they have to ask how these could be considered the Word of God.

Must we believe, for example, that within families and in society at large males are to be dominant, females subordinate? Should women, as was taught by certain church spokesmen whose writings made their way into this New Testament, be "silent in the churches," with no permission to "teach or to have authority over a man"?[4] Was it ever right that some humans should be able to own and make use of other humans, as slaves, for personal comfort and economic security and profit?

And what kind of a God is it who would bring about the death of the Egyptian firstborn—by "hardening the heart" of Egypt's ruler? Or declare to Moses that "the Lord will have war with Amalek from generation to generation" and "will utterly blot out the remembrance of Amalek from under heaven"?[5]

Must God be worshiped by the women of our day under the predominantly male imagery of "king," "father," or "husband"—especially when some of the images associated with sinful humanity seem to degrade not just female persons but femaleness itself?

Are we to accept an interpretation of Scripture, from later times, that sees God as "Father" arranging, so to speak, the execution of his "Son"—as sinless "substitute"—in order that for God the "judge" the full penalty of the law could be exacted? And must we then go on to declare that it is only through an explicit profession of faith in this saving act of God in Jesus that anyone can know God as reconciler and liberator—thereby endangering (for "eternity") the great majority of human beings who have existed on this planet?[6]

Where does "fundamentalism" fit into this picture?

Even people who take little notice of religion are aware of believers spoken of as biblical "fundamentalists" for whom the upholding of their faith depends on a "literal" reading of Holy Scripture.[7] The term "literal" points to a principle essential to the consideration of any sort of belief: namely, that all dealings with texts involve the act of interpretation. The long dispute between so-called "fundamentalists" and "liberals" within the Christian church arises from differing approaches to the interpretation of the "letters," so to speak (Latin: *litterae*), making up the biblical texts. The conflict is not between "Bible-believing" churches and other church groups that don't believe the Bible. It is between different ways of listening for the "word of God" in and through the words of that Bible.

Or, to say the same thing in other terms, different beliefs about the "authority" of Holy Scripture. Those for whom the Bible has authority read its stories and sayings and poetic utterances in order to govern their lives thereby. The question is whether a conclusion about what "the Bible says . . ." always warrants the assertion "God says . . . ."

Interpretation, though, involves history. And the uses of language. If these texts from such earlier times and from cultures so different from ours are to address the needs of our time, their language must be adequately understood. This requires attention to historical context: we need to know what meanings certain words written in that language might have conveyed to those for whom they were originally written.

Historical context involves another issue as well: In this act of interpretive reading, are we to allow also for the differences between that "world" and our own time and place? Must we address the text from our historical situation and worldview as well as from what we have learned of the history behind the ancient writing?

Can we read the Genesis creation stories, for example, without taking account of differences between a scientific and a pre-scientific understanding of reality? Would it make any difference to followers of Jesus if many of the details in the gospel accounts of Jesus' suffering and death were found by historians to derive not from eyewitness testimony but from creative reflection on certain texts from the Old Testament? Does the book of Revelation become irrelevant if its images and its symbolic narrative are not necessarily about events bringing about the "end of the world"?

Biblical fundamentalists would want to insist that modern readers find their way into the world of the Bible, rather than that the biblical content also be reconsidered in light of contemporary ways of thinking. For those Scriptures, without which we could not receive God's self-revelation, are taken to be—through the gift of "inspiration"—without error. Interpretations may be flawed, but the writings themselves, in this view, are the "Word of God" and, therefore, like God's own self, perfect.

It would follow that none of the Bible's teachings are, as the "liberals" say, historically relative ("They thought that way in those days; we have a different worldview now"). These truths would have to be timeless truths, and the morality laid down thereby an absolute morality.[8] Which helps to explain why fundamentalists continue to support the teaching of "creationism" rather than evolution in the schools, why they put forth such efforts in support of the so-called "traditional" family and those sexual behaviors allegedly sanctioned by Holy Scripture, and why so many of them expect a "second coming" in which Jesus will actually descend from the heavens to take true believers home and bring on the "end of the world."[9]

Fundamentalists would argue, then, that a "yes" to God would entail also something close to an "absolute" "yes" to the collection of ancient texts we call Holy Scripture—a "yes" to its stories as fact, no matter how their details seem to be contradicted by historical research and scientific theory; a "yes" to its values as right, no matter how much some of those values outrage our modern habits of thought.

Their liberal opponents have insisted that believers can say "yes" to modern ways of understanding scientific and historical truth and say "no," accordingly, to much of the traditional way of approaching the Bible. They are willing to read the stories of creation and flood as "myths," to deliteralize miracle stories, and to disown the violence and war and ethnic prejudice characterizing many of the stories told about Israel's history. Some might pass lightly over certain interpretations of Jesus' death and that mysterious happening the New Testament speaks of as his "resurrection," and debunk a number of the beliefs and attitudes found in the letters of the Apostle Paul—and almost certainly dismiss certain traditional ways of reading the Revelation to John.

Fundamentalism is attractive to those seeking an assured ground for faith; but it can also be hazardous to faith. From its pre-modern worldview, language which seems to demand to be read as metaphor and symbol is treated, instead, as matter of fact. Stories of wonders, or "miracles," are "taken straight," with no room allowed for the intrusion of legendary elements traceable to ancient understandings of the relationship between God and created nature.

When the sayings or stories have to do with concerns such as the roles of women and men, sexual behavior, the morality of war, or the function of government in matters having to do with what we now speak of as "values"[10] such "literal" readings can prompt serious questions about the attitudes of believers embracing these interpretations and the attributes of the God to whom they declare allegiance.

A larger worldview question may be raised as well: If this God of the Bible is in full relationship with the world which Christians take to be God's creation, is it not likely that developments in human culture and society—including new understandings of reality and new practical uses of such knowledge—will involve not just human perversity and error but also divine guidance leading to truer knowledge of God's creation and wiser ways of living together on earth?

Why not read the Bible, in that case, as dramatizing the negotiations between a God who offers possibilities appropriate to a particular place and time and the gifted but flawed human partners who both receive and reject—and reshape—what is offered? And why not accept the written witness to that interaction as the "mixed bag" it clearly is and make the sorting out of its contents part of the divine-human partnership?

But "liberal" approaches to Scripture—this has also to be said—can be equally hazardous to faith. Those too ready to accommodate the messages of the Bible to modern ways of thinking may "water down" the biblical witness to the divine-human journey through time to such a degree that followers of the way of God as taught by and embodied in Jesus become virtually indistinguishable from modern non-believing secularists: not much more, it could be said, than "nice" people with a vague sense that God and Jesus have something to do with their "niceness."

To them, too, a challenge must be addressed: Shouldn't we expect biblical stories and sayings to exert pressure on the beliefs and practices we tend to take for granted as "modern" people, even as those modern patterns of thought and behavior call into question certain traditional approaches to the ancient texts?

Is there another way to remain attuned to the biblical witness to God's dealings with humankind? Can we be sensitive at one and the same time to the ancientness of the texts and to the modernity of our own frame of reference? Can we learn to say both "yes" *and* "no" to the question: "Is the Bible the 'Word of God'?"

Can we say "yes" to truth that isn't necessarily "fact"?

Let us start with Jesus, focusing not on the question of whether or not this or that action, saying, or event associated with his memory actually happened but on the issue of what it meant (and means) that *Jesus* "happened," that the whole complex event called "Jesus" took place.

Suppose we ask not how many facts we can authenticate but how much truth we have been given as to who Jesus was. Suppose the Gospels, even if they cannot give us the for-sure words of Jesus, cause us to hear (as someone has suggested) the authentic "voice" of Jesus. As for the stories—what if the issue concerns not our accepting all the *words about* Jesus, but our accepting of Jesus *as "Word,"* as the crucified-and-risen one in whom believers see God and their own fully-realized humanity?

Through such a reading, those remembered facts and that reconstructed history—and even the additional stories overflowing from inspired, faith-full imaginations—can put us in touch with that living truth and that healing presence, now, in this new millennium, just as surely as walking into Capernaum nearly two thousand years ago could bring a Galilean peasant or rich landowner before the real-life fact named Jesus.

So it can be also with regard to the many narratives of the Old Testament that fail the fact-test for truth. There are facts at the core of the story. To say that Judaism—and the Christianity developing out of Jewish belief—are historical religions is to insist that such a faith centers on something that "happened" between God and human beings, thereby making possible comparable things that happen, now, for persons putting their faith in that God.

But how do the stories clustering around such central narratives get told? Not necessarily with a fine regard for what we would consider fact, even though there would have been a great concern for what we are asked to consider truth. What happened to the runaways who later became the people Israel was attributed to God. Therefore their escape from Egypt and their journey toward Canaan had to be accompanied with "wonders" witnessing to divine presence—like the crossing, on dry land, through the "Sea of Reeds" and the provision of manna from nowhere and water from the rock.[11]

Such stories do the work of metaphors. Accordingly, stories like these don't mean: You, too, can walk through a body of water without drowning, or find delicate sweet food available with every morning's dew, or slake your thirst by beating on limestone with a staff. They mean: God will be with you (*is* with you, now!) even in seemingly impossible crises, and God can satisfy the heart's deepest needs: that's the way God is, that's what it's like to walk with God in faith.[12]

Can we say "yes" despite teachings felt to be not "right"?

The historical limitations of the lawgivers and prophets and sages—and the apostles and evangelists, as well—who gave us these ancient texts concerned not only their understandings of what can be held to be *true,* but also their beliefs as to what can be taken, in terms of human behavior, as *right.*

Accordingly, as already mentioned, numerous passages in the Bible advocate male dominance as the divinely-ordained state of things, or consider slaveholding an acceptable practice, or recommend wholesale slaughter in the name of a holy God. What is perhaps not so broadly grasped is that numerous other biblical passages open up visions greatly at variance with views such as those just glanced at. By way of what Christian believers would take to be the "promptings" of the Holy Spirit, visions are offered of new possibilities for human life in community.

A helpful image for grasping this reality comes to us from theologian Burton Cooper's book *Why, God?* The image is that of a "deep coal mine with many seams, some of which are rich with coal, others . . . not." The Bible can be thought of that way, Cooper suggests, "with seams we have been mining for centuries and others we have hardly touched."[13]

So it is that the Bible offers alternative images and stories of God as well as those so often found objectionable. The "almighty" God presented as visiting "plagues" on the stubbornly resistant Egyptians and slaughtering those among God's "own people" who turn to pagan ways is also the God depicted by some of the prophets as a loving parent agonizing over the self-destructive wilfulness of beloved children. The Gospels envision a Jesus who weeps over a doomed Jerusalem and faithfully endures humiliation and pain at the hands of a hate-filled power elite.

The God who in some parts of the Bible is a very masculine "father" and "Lord" can be seen elsewhere (Psalm 103, for example) as a father not characterized by unbending autocratic ways but filled with tenderness. Or as not "father" at all but as a mother who could never "forget her nursing child," never fail to show "compassion for the child of her womb."[14] Though the movers and shakers of Israel's history are mostly male figures, Old Testament writings also present a remarkable number of women (the likes of Miriam, Deborah, Ruth, the prophetess Huldah, and others) to be reckoned with for their contributions to that same history.

And Jesus? Jesus is remembered in the Gospels as one who freely welcomed women into his circle. Even the apostle Paul, the same Paul who apparently spoke up for male supremacy and condoned slavery, is heard to declare that for those who are "one in Christ Jesus" "there is no longer Jew or Greek, there is no longer slave or free, there is no longer male and female."[15]

This was happening for Paul—and it keeps happening for us, Christians would affirm—because of Jesus. There was in that event constituted by Jesus' life and death and entrance into risen life in God something essentially transformative, something that was and is, in Paul's words, a "new creation."

Through that same Spirit, such transformative promptings can come likewise by non-biblical channels: through philosophers, novelists and poets, historians, researchers in psychology and anthropology, and many others contemplating the human condition—none of them claiming, or needing to claim, the sanction of any religious body.

Through non-Christian *religious* channels as well: observant Judaism, Eastern wisdom, the rigorous truths of Islam, the creation spirituality of the Native American heritage.[16] For all that feeds the answers to our persistent questions about our own humanity can help us in the reading of those texts that specifically put us in touch with the God, known in Jesus, who has promised abundant life in a world undergoing transformation.

No, the Bible—if it is read word by word, image by image, idea by idea without reference to history—is not as such the "Word of God." As William Sloane Coffin has pointed out, in such readings the Bible is often used the way a drunk uses a lamppost—more for support than for illumination! And yes, the Bible—if it is read as the product of a continuing, changing relationship through time—can yield to its readers, again and again, a "Word of God."

What will we need to do to make a "yes-*and*-no" response to the Bible work for us?

How can we come to be both receptive to and critical of the narratives and poetry and wisdom teachings of Holy Scripture? How can we say the kind of "yes *and* no" already advocated and still be saying "I *don't* mean maybe!"?

First, we will have to *read* the book. More accurately, read *in* the book. Since not everything the Bible presents is of equal interest or equal value, a straight-through, chapter-by-chapter campaign is not advisable. Even the most motivated reader tends to bog down somewhere in Exodus and to stay that way until part-way through Numbers! But we must read this so-holy-and-so-human book, if for nothing else than to experience its moments of self-authenticating power. For many are the women and men who have found the reading of a parable of Jesus, or a sentence in the prophets, or a passage from Paul's letters an arresting, even a life-changing experience.

We may have to read with *helps*. The use of something like a "study Bible" is not an indication of weakness, either on the part of the reader or the book. For any ancient text—an epic of Homer, Hinduism's *Bhagavad Gita*, Dante's *Divine Comedy*—most of us need some guidance if we are to find ourselves sufficiently at home in that "other world" to have a context for interpretation.

We should stop frequently to *reflect*, even to "meditate," on some narrative or passage of poetry that has caught our attention. Meditation on the experienced meanings concentrated in an aphorism or a poetic image or an economically-told story can release astonishing quantities of spiritual insight. The effect can be compared with the phenomena of implosion and explosion. A great deal of energy compressed in a small space is "imploded" energy. What happens when something is done to release that energy is that sudden, intense, wide-ranging event called an "explosion."

We have to take on the task of *interpreting* the texts of the Bible, as well, interpreting them with a full recognition of the various "seams" to be found in the text itself as well as the changes such interpreting goes through as human consciousness undergoes its own changes. New trends in interpretation often manifest the patient working of this same Spirit of God nudging us toward a "re-reading" of our world in light of a re-interpreting of Scripture—or a reinterpretation of Holy Scripture in light of new re-readings of our world. One contemporary instance of this process is the emergence in a number of religious bodies of a "women's movement" which has as one of its goals the freeing of women from the Bible-based oppression that has been termed, wittily, "textual harassment."[17]

What grounds our "yes *and* no" to the Bible in a deeper "I *don't* mean maybe!"?

"One does not live by bread alone," Deuteronomy tells us, "but by every word that comes from the mouth of the Lord."[18] "Word" takes in, of course, all those elements in human experience which can be signs of divine presence. But it must be understood as referring, also, to the written words of the Bible, whereby we are enabled to discern the ultimate meaning of all these signs and test our story by that larger story to which the Bible is witness.

Opportunities for this testing of our story are constantly on offer.

For many, such opportunities come by way of our culture. The stories it tells and the images it projects—in poems, books, films, TV programs, newspaper articles—convey aspects of the story which helped make this, however problematically, a Christian society. The role played by church programs of worship and study has already been mentioned.

In the endeavor to hear the word of God through the words of the biblical text, we can learn to rest in our relationship with the God who speaks that Word and who has come to us, as the embodied Word, in Jesus. This enables us to say not just "yes *and* no" but, also, "I *don't* mean maybe!"—in the assurance Paul gives that as we "work out [our] own salvation with fear and trembling," "it is [at the same time] God who is at work in [us], enabling [us] both to will and to work for [God's] good pleasure."[19]

We don't have to get stuck, then, with reading the Bible as a book *about* God; we can learn to read it—as Gabriel Josipovici urges, by way of the very title of his 1988 publication *The Book of God*[20]—not seeking to gain, as it were, the "facts" needed for understanding the ways of God, but seeking to learn *from* God in our journey through, and visits with, this "book of God."

Because they position their practice of faith within a belief system that is both narrow and rigid, people in both fundamentalist and liberal camps are always in danger of becoming intolerant of other ways of believing. Sometimes the focus of a fundamentalist interest in Scripture is particularly restricted—to questions of race, for instance, or sexuality, or abortion, or supposed prophecies concerning the end of the world—and the interpretations are especially dogmatic. That's when fundamentalism can turn bizarre, or hateful, even deadly. And that, more often than not, is when the TV cameras will appear—and the reporters with their notebooks—and the stereotypical pictures and stories so damaging not only to literalist readers but to all who take the Bible seriously.[21]

The biblical literalists I myself have known have been persons committed to a life walk with a God of holiness and love, even if some of their beliefs tended to shut them off from too many others sharing that same intention. And some of the supposedly broad-minded liberals I have known have been as contemptuous in their way as their narrower-minded fellow-religionists. To people in both camps the words of J. B. Phillips, in the title of a book written many years ago now, can speak a much-needed truth: "Your God is too small."[22]

As long as all who desire the stories and images and teachings of the Bible to influence their walk with God also desire to remain grounded in the love of that God with whom we make our way through life, we will be able to continue hurling our interpretive "yeses" and "noes" at one another without losing confidence in our shared communion, our commonly held "yes and I *don't* mean maybe!" to divine wisdom and love.

A moment from a movie of recent years can speak to this concern. Sonny (played by Robert Duvall) is a non-denominational, revivalist ("the Bible says . . .") kind of preacher who calls himself—in a term that also gives the movie its title—the "apostle." In the scene referred to, Sonny is watching a priest in Louisiana blessing a fleet of shrimp boats. As the "apostle"—who is always in open shirt and casual pants and always preaches "as the Spirit leads him"—takes in the ornate vestments of the cleric and his set prayers-from-the-book, he chuckles, and then declares: "Well, you do it your way and I do it mine. But we get it done!"

ENDNOTES

[1] Many and varied writings emerged in the early Christian movement. Of these, twenty-seven came to be chosen, over a considerable time, as "scripture"—authoritative for the church's faith and life—the criteria being (supposed) apostolic origin and acceptably "orthodox" teaching. With regard to use of the terms "Old" and "New" Testament, see note 23 in Chapter One.

[2] Joshua chapter 6.

[3] The "Jesus Seminar," a group of scholars specializing in New Testament writings, mainly the gospels, have attracted considerable attention through their practice of seeking to determine—by their particular methods of research and in the form, ultimately, of voting (with colored beads)—which sayings and acts of Jesus are likely to be "authentic"; that is, to have actually been said or done by Jesus rather than attributed to him by later interpreters.

[4] 1 Corinthians 14:34; 1 Timothy 2:11-12.

[5] References are to Exodus 11:10 and 17:14-16.

[6] Very much to the point is the humorously sarcastic "explanation" of these teachings by the English writer Dorothy Sayers: "God wanted to damn everybody, but his vindictive sadism was sated by the crucifixion of his own Son, who was quite innocent, and, therefore, a particularly attractive victim. He now only damns people who don't follow Christ or have never heard of him." *Christian Letters to a Post Christian World* (Grand Rapids: Wm. B. Eerdmans Pub. Co., 1969), cited in Douglas John Hall, *Professing the Faith: Christian Theology in a North American Context* (Minneapolis: Fortress Press, 1993), 425n.2.

[7] Historically, and more comprehensively, the term "fundamentalism" derives from the publication, between 1910 and 1915, of a series of booklets—called *The Fundamentals*—upholding certain elements of traditional teaching held to be "fundamental" to authentic Christian faith.

[8] Jurgen Moltmann, "Liberalism and Fundamentalism in the Modern Era," in *God for a Secular Society: The Public Relevance of Theology* (Minneapolis: Fortress Press, 1999), 217.

[9] I can recall, from earlier years spent in churches with fundamentalist tendencies, classes on Revelation and Daniel in which hand-drawn charts were used to show

when and how various predictive images were to be fulfilled, and a session on the creation stories in Genesis in which the leader was earnestly explaining how "fossils" had been divinely placed within the geologic folds of the earth.

A recent manifestation of end-of-the-world literalism is the best-selling "Left Behind" series by Tim LaHaye and Jerry Jenkins, books which turn those allegedly predictive images into fictional page-turners.

[10] Politically, fundamentalist Christians are often behind legislative initiatives in opposition to homosexual rights, abortion, and the teaching of evolution in school curriculums and in support of prayer in schools and the posting of the Ten Commandments in public places.

[11] References are to Exodus chapter 14, with 15:4 (Scholars point out that the body of water crossed is called in Hebrew the "Sea of Reeds"—not the Red Sea of popular memory but a shallow body of water further north), and chapters 16 and 17.

[12] This metaphorical approach to the reading of the Bible is developed helpfully in Marcus J. Borg's *Reading the Bible Again for the First Time: Taking the Bible Seriously but Not Literally* (HarperSanFrancisco, 2001).

[13] Burton Z. Cooper, *Why, God?* (Atlanta: John Knox Press, 1988), 45.

[14] Isaiah 49:14-15.

[15] Galatians 3:28. Also to be noted is the large number of women's names in the greetings extended by the Apostle Paul in chapter 16 of his Letter to the Romans

[16] One of the most accessible introductions to the various major religions is Huston Smith's *The World's Religions* (HarperSanFrancisco, 1991).

[17] A phrase coined by Mary Jacobus and used, as a section heading, in Peter Gomes, The *Good Book: Reading the Bible with Mind and Heart* (New York: William Morrow, 1996), 135.

[18] Deuteronomy 8:3.

[19] Philippians 2:12-13.

[20] Gabriel Josipovici, *The Book of God: A Response to the Bible* (New Haven: Yale University Press, 1988).

[21] The topic is dealt with at length in Nancy Ammerman's "North American Protestant Fundamentalism," in *Fundamentalisms Observed,*, ed. Martin E. Marty and R. Scott Appleby (Chicago and London: University of Chicago Press, 1991), 1-65

[22] J. B. Phillips, *Your God Is Too Small* (New York: Simon and Schuster, Touchstone ed., 1997).

CHAPTER THREE

Is God "in Control"? Questions about God as Creator and Provider

"He's got the whole world," we sing, "in his hands." "He's got the sisters and the brothers in his hands.""He's got the little bitty baby in his hands." And more, much more, of the same. For if we can know God, we want to know that God as one who guarantees order in the world. More than that, our troubled hearts demand a God who will *save us*—save me! mine!—from personal disaster. At times, even the most "secular" and skeptical persons will find themselves pleading with that "something out there," to "save us!"

But can we sing, "He's got the great big hurricane in his hands"? Or: "He's got the DNA in his hands"? Or "He's got the ethnic cleansers—and the terrorist bombers—in his hands"?*Is* God, as the spiritual would suggest, "in control"?

For those in the path of a hurricane, or in an area overrun by terrorist militias, or watching the blazing towers fall in upon themselves, the question is not at all speculative; it erupts from a heart and mind "perplexed in the extreme." And, of course, there are other threats. A child is born; but, instead of family-wide celebration there is anxious waiting, followed by great sadness, as serious defects of body and mind presage years of unremitting effort and expense. Clinical depression shadows someone whose only "sin" is having a body/mind with a certain chemical imbalance.

"Where was God," people ask, "when that horror struck? If God has 'got the whole world in his hands,' why do disasters like this come upon us?"

All such questioning presupposes the possibility of a God we can believe in, one guaranteeing order in the universe. Many people become "practicing atheists" and stop asking these questions about God precisely because for them the evidence all points to disorder, to lack of control.

I spoke with a woman, some years ago, whose son had committed suicide by driving his car into a nearby river. I was at her front door representing the church this woman had once attended with some regularity. But she told me—coldly, resentfully, through the screen door—"Since my son died, the man upstairs and I don't get along so well."

Some of us, however, can't keep from asking these questions, despite disappointing "answers" supposedly received. We can't help returning to the places of hurt to reexamine our questioning and our range of available answers. This chapter invites such wounded questers and questioners to consider whether the query "Is God in control?" can be answered "yes *and* no" without dissolving answer and question into nonsense or irrelevancy.

Questions to be considered in this chapter include the following:

- How does this issue relate to the traditional belief in God as creator and provider? Is there a necessary conflict, here, between science and religion?
- How does our creativity as human beings figure in the divine creating and providing?
- What would characterize an existence carried on as if God *is* "in control" as creator and provider? What does it mean to say that we are "creatures of God"?
- Given the prevalence of catastrophic "evils," can we say that God is "in control" of "Nature"? Would such "control" mean that "miracles" happen?
- Given the prevalence of suffering caused by human beings, can we say that God is "in control" of the human will?
- Does God have competition for control—an opposing spiritual reality called "Satan"?
- How *is* divine control exercised in the world? What is God's role? What is ours?
- How can we reconcile a belief in God's "control" with our own ultimate loss of control: our dying?

Is God "in control" as Creator and Provider

A larger question underlies this issue of divine power as understood, by many, in terms of "control": What is the relationship between God and this "natural" world we take to be the context for our human existence? The Christian answer asks us to view the world as God's "creation." For Christians affirm first of all—as do Jews and Muslims, for that matter—that God's "got the whole world in his hands" as its *creator* and *provider*.

The question for this chapter, then, has to be considered in relation to that belief in God as creator and provider. What sort of system is it—this realm of "nature" and this human world—in which human and non-human entities come into being, continue their various terms of existence, and, soon or late, perish? What role does God play, in relation to this system? Can we legitimately ask "Is God in control?" And, if God *is* in any way present to the world as its creator and provider, what should be our response?

The answer to the question of creation is "no" if the terms reached for are merely those of modern scientific theorizing. For all such theorizing proceeds from questions that begin with the word "how?" And the hypotheses suggesting answers tend to limit themselves to strictly material, not "spiritual," causes.

It all started, say many scientists of our time, in a first brief flash nicknamed the "Big Bang." And the history of the cosmos has unfolded by way of a process first identified by nineteenth-century scientific observers and thinkers as Evolution.

This is as it should be. Asking and answering the "how" questions is what science is for; and it is not what religion is for. When a conflict develops, it is because certain religious believers insist on answering questions about *how* new forms of being appear and develop through a literal reading of very ancient texts, or because certain scientific thinkers insist that *their* answers to questions of how things come to be and continue in being can satisfy other questions human beings desire to address as well to this unfathomable mystery.[1] As Albert Einstein has rightly said, "Science without religion is lame. Religion without science is blind."[2]

But a "yes" can be said, as well, to the question "Is God creator and provider?" if Christian teaching about creation is taken to be not an explanation but an affirmation. For what such an article of belief would insist is that everywhere, always, we know ourselves to be confronted with ultimate mystery, in this case an ultimate *creative and sustaining* mystery.

The classic opening words of the book of Genesis announce that "in the beginning God created the heavens and the earth." But the question to which those words provide an answer is not: How, by what measurable processes, did everything come into being? The question is, rather: To what deepest reality is everything finally related? To affirm God as creator is to declare, in faith, that we owe our existence to God, are upheld in being by God, are destined for God, and are involved with one another in a unity of being deriving from our shared relation with God.

The language for such an understanding of reality would have to be that of metaphor and story. In groping toward something we don't understand, we reach for something we think we do know and set it side by side with the mystifying term, in the language transaction called metaphor. And story? This is our most basic way of setting forth the possible connections among these glimpsed realities and the significance of that pattern for our life in the world.

A belief in God as "creator and provider," then, would be another metaphoric way of reaching into mystery, another way of connecting such "dots" as we have into a particular "figure" that helps satisfy certain profound needs of mind and heart and permits us to grapple with certain related questions in our lives.

Perhaps the most significant and helpful image for God's creative work in the cosmos is that which dominates the creation story found in Genesis chapter l: the image of speech. Into the "formless void and darkness" of the "beginning" a word is spoken: God says, "Let there be light." And then? "There was light." For each of the ensuing creative actions the formula is essentially the same: "And God said . . ." "And it was so." This is a God (according to the Apostle Paul) who "calls into existence the things that do not exist."[3]

But this metaphor of God's speaking things into being speaking can be more broadly interpreted. It can be understood as going on in a more "democratic" cosmos, so to speak—not so much by edict, that is, but by invitation and urging. God-the-creator can be pictured, then, as the ever-and-everywhere-present urge or intention whereby all the multitudinous creative forces are put to work and sustained.

The writer D. H. Lawrence reaches toward such an image, in a humorous but serious poem about some favorite contrasting flowers that provide him his title: "Red Geranium and Godly Mignonette." Scoffing lightheartedly at the notion that the "Most High" could have thought out "in the abstract, when all was twilit green and muddy:"

> 'Now there shall be tum-tiddly-um, and tum-tiddly-um,
> hey—presto! scarlet geranium!'

the poet suggests a more satisfying imaginal alternative: "Imagine," he says,

> among the mud and the mastodons
> God sighing and yearning with tremendous creative
> yearning, in that dark green mess
> oh, for some other beauty, some other beauty
> that blossomed at last, red geranium, and mignonette.[4]

Not a God-as-magician, then, working from "outside" (as we say) to draw galaxies from hats or to make wildflowers appear where previously we saw nothing, but God as visionary artist, working "from within," and by way of creative processes themselves evoked by divine creative desire, to welcome into the world constantly new forms and possibilities of being.

We could say, then, that taking in the "picture thinking," as theologian James McClendon calls it, of the biblical writings concerning first things is like "interviewing" such an artist. We won't get from our encounter the full truth as to how the artist produced the painting or symphony or poem, but we can go away with some sense of how the artist works, and to what end, and in what spirit.

A God involved—lovingly, unwaveringly—in the process by which new realities emerge has to be understood also as *providing for* the ongoing existence of these structures and life forms.

This theme as well is present from the Bible's very first page. In the story-liturgy of Genesis chapter 1 and the second creation account, in chapter 2, basic sustenance is offered ("Every plant yielding seed . . . and every tree with seed in its fruit; you shall have them for food"). But provision is also made for other gifts, those that render life human as well as merely creaturely.

Companionship. "It is not good," says the voice in this folktale about human origins, "that the man should be alone; I will make him a helper as his partner." *Language*, as well. *Vocation*. There is work to be done—valuable, dignified work: humans are given "dominion over . . . every living thing that moves upon the earth" and placed in the garden to "till it and keep it." *Rest*: the rhythmic alternation of labor and rest, by way of the sabbath, that "seventh day" "hallowed" by God.[5]

The most important provision of all, though easily passed over by "secular" readers, is the *presence* of God as companion and guide—and as conversation partner. From first page to last in the biblical narrative we are made aware of that presence and let in on that conversation.

Something else has to be said as well: God not only creates creatures, God creates *creativity*. Creation—or creativity—continues partly through the ingenuity of human beings inspired by God to invent the tools and skills and ordered procedures of mind and hand that constitute human culture and make possible human society.

Can we live in the world *as if* God's "got the whole world in his hands"?

How should we live, then, as creatures of God, in relation to the realm we call "nature," in relation to other human beings as fellow creatures, and in that inner communion which is individual consciousness?

First (biblical visions suggest), we could live *trustfully*—with what psychologist Erik Erikson spoke of as "basic trust"—assured that in our beginning and at our end and in all that comes between, God is present.[6]

Second, we could live *expectantly*. Creation means the emergence of what is new. All is dark, formless, empty—chaotic. Then—"Light!" "Let there be light!" How often for us some "formless void and darkness," has given way, unexpectedly, creatively, to a glimmer or a great shining that is unmistakably of God.[7]

We could learn to live *appreciatively*, giving praise for the grace that creates and provides. For the poet Dylan Thomas, each of the Genesis creation events is itself an expression of awestruck thankfulness. And so, in one of his poems, he imagines

> the spellbound horses walking warm
> Out of the whinnying green stable
> On to the fields of praise.[8]

And why not live *festively* in God's creation, enjoying what we are as God's workmanship and what we can touch, hear, and see all around us? The Genesis 1 story suggests—in the repeated words "And God saw that it was good"—that this is God's own response to everything God creates. "Goodness" here has to do not with moral worth but with beauty, with (so to speak) artistic rightness. God here is the painter stepping back to appraise the most recent brush strokes or the poet reading a few lines aloud to enjoy the "feel" of them.

Living *communally* is something we *must* learn: living with and for our fellow creatures. Our being is always a being-*with*, whether in comradely endeavor, or the varying degrees of friendship, or love expressed also through our sexuality, or solicitous care given and received.

With God our creator and provider "in control," in the ways already suggested, we can learn also to live *productively*, as faithful *co*-creators and *co*-providers with God. The Spirit of God, as "expressed" in the "Word-made-flesh" Jesus Christ, continues the divine work of creating a world and providing for it, as we respond not only to our social vocation but also to the ecological imperative which calls us to be both partners with all that is and, in certain aspects, stewards of the enterprise of being as well.

All this means that we can, and must, learn to live a *creaturely* existence, embracing both the glorious freedoms that are ours and the salutary limits. Life is rich with opportunities for our "yes"—invitations to partake, enjoy, name, make use of—but also with prohibitions requiring a "no" or a "yes, but."

One last creaturely limit has also to be kept in mind: our mortality. We are all destined to "return to the ground" out of which we were taken.[9] As poet Mary Oliver reminds us, in her poem "In Blackwater Woods,"

> To live in this world
> you must be able
> to do three things:
> to love what is mortal,
> to hold it
>
> against your bones knowing
> your own life depends on it,
> and, when the time comes to let it go,
> to let it go.[10]

Must we say "No" as well as "Yes" to the question: Is God "in control"?

Such a "no" would have to be spoken at this point, to protest the apparent screening out—in this visionary "as-if" presentation—of the shadow side of life on earth.

It is all very well to speak of trust and, like Jesus, seek to emulate the lilies of the field and the birds of the air; but what of human beings whose circumstances more than justify a deep and chronic anxiety? How can we expect refugee infants or babies born to famine-ravaged mothers to gain the "basic trust" so essential to the navigation of ensuing life passages?

And what of the energies in nature that are monstrous? Will we praise the orderedness of things when our house is directly in the path of the funnel-shaped cloud or towering tsunami, or when infinitely tiny energy-nodes inside the cells of a body forming within a womb can consign that new being to a radically limited mode of existence?

Is human community something to rejoice in if tribal enmities or racial prejudice or religious fanaticism can breed bloody massacres and campaigns for "ethnic cleansing"? What are we to make of a supposedly God-given creativity whose great achievement is a technologically advanced, meticulously managed "final solution" taking the form of death camps for the wiping out of a whole generation of Jews and other "undesirables"?

Where is God, people ask, where is God when such catastrophic things are happening? Or—the chief question for this chapter:—*What* is God that such things *can* happen? Is God "in control" or not?

Is God "in control" of "Nature"?

Mention has been made of "evils" such as earthquakes, floods, and anomalous sudden illnesses which are often called "natural." What could God have to do, as creator and provider, with these arbitrary incursions of disorder and destruction?

As already suggested, there seems to be a kind of "openness," or randomness, in created nature that resembles the sense we have as humans of our personal freedom. Regularities—order, predictability—seem to have the upper hand; but "disorderings" are plentiful, as well, catastrophes like those mentioned already and other breakdowns which result from actions of human creatures who destroy forests, or pour noxious fumes into the atmosphere, or build in areas susceptible to flooding or earthquakes.

Is God "in control" of nature? The answer would have to be "no," if what is looked for is absolute sovereignty—unless we are ready to assert, with our unqualified "yes," that the loving, all-powerful God thus envisioned would deliberately "send" such suffering on multitudes of decent, unprepared people.

A "yes-*and*-no" answer, in contrast, would affirm the general provision of God for the unimaginably intricate web of the natural creation, but it would also point out the apparent constraints on divine freedom over against the occasionally disruptive "freedoms" of winds, and ocean currents, and tectonic plates, and cell structure. This could explain the "no" part of such an answer. The question would still remain—and is to be taken up in the last part of this chapter—as to what the "yes" part could entail.

But first—by way of a parenthesis—a brief consideration of a topic not to be evaded if any attention at all is being given to traditions of Christian belief.

(Parenthesis:) God's "Control" and the Question of "Miracles"

Can God "do miracles"? No, if miracle means—as it still does, for many—something like a "suspension of natural law." People holding such a belief will want to say that if God is "maker of heaven and earth," God "can do anything," can even say, on certain occasions, "Forget the rules; let's do it *this* way."

And sometimes—oh, how we want it to be so! If only it could be, as in the games of children, that as much magic as needed was immediately to hand! For some people, in fact, praying is invoking something like magic. We have all heard on news programs those soundbite interviews with people in the path of flood waters, or parents in the hospital waitingroom after the surgery: "Well, we've done what could be done. All we can do now is pray."

But why not? The Bible itself is full of such stories, stories of people in extremity, desperately praying for rescue. Stories, even, of nature's "rules" set aside for particular outbreaks of divine power: Jesus walking on the water, for example, or stilling a storm, or turning water into wine.

Why? What is something like the walking-on-water story in Mark chapter 6 doing there? What can it mean for us? Gospel accounts suggest that almost all the "wonders" performed by Jesus were for the sake of persons directly in need, and were related to natural processes of body and mind only dimly understood in that time and still largely mysterious. Stories about "nature" miracles, then, could have developed later. With a growing conviction that to know Jesus was, in some sense, to know God would come the tendency to ascribe to Jesus powers traditionally associated with the workings of an almighty God in the world.

But, as Old Testament scholar Terence Fretheim insists, God's "acts" in the world may involve the "extraordinary" without thereby constituting "interventions" in nature's regularities. The divine work is being done through means provided (in Fretheim's terms) by the "causal continuum"—but there can be sufficient "play" in that network of causes for the happily unexpected to occur.[11]

We can also say "yes," then, to the question about miracles. But we need not imagine such happenings as an overruling of nature's laws. God is acting within nature, but is perceived as acting so "vividly"—as McClendon puts it in his consideration of this topic—that the divine intention is thereby displayed, and God's presence made to shine forth for creative and redemptive ends.[12]

We are not to misrepresent either the "laws" of nature or the freedom of God. I heard once of a religious young man who—taking up a literalistic reading of the story (in 2 Kings chapter 4) describing the prophet Elisha's resuscitation of the Shunnamite's son—stretched himself out (imitating Elisha) on the still-warm corpse of his father seeking to bring him back to life. Needless to say, it didn't "work." We must not presume. Rules continue to be rules.

But we must not fall, either, into an undervaluing of the power of God. God continues to be God. (And we don't know everything about the "rules"!) I was myself the subject, at age eleven, of an unexpected healing taking place in the context of urgent, communal prayer. And many readers will be able to add their own stories of comparable "miracles."[13] We have every right, as people of faith, to believe in—and claim (even while not presuming on!)—the loving power of a God who enables "signs and wonders."

Is God "in control" of the human will?

It is too often forgotten that God is not "in control" of the human will. We are free, both to respond faithfully to what we sense to be God's best for us—thereby allowing God to be, for us at that moment, "in control"—and to assert ourselves in ways counter to the divine intention. Such contrary actions and the dispositions behind them belong under the heading of "sin." There can be sinful impulses so pervasive and so intense that they erupt among masses of people and result in the oppression, even destruction, of hundreds of thousands, millions: the Holocaust of Hitler's Europe and the slaughter of so many thousands in central Africa, as well as those subtler, longer-term, lower-intensity atrocities associated with White America's racism, and the system of Apartheid set aside not long ago in South Africa, and massive terrorist acts done in the name of religion.

In each case, a false god has been enthroned: racial or ethnic superiority or slavish belief in a particular ideology. Our own emerging ideology, perhaps, of consumerist free-market "economism," exploiting masses of people in the pursuit of unprecedented prosperity for the relatively few. Exploiting the environment, as well, thereby bequeathing to later generations dangerous scarcities of essentials like water, along with life-threatening pollution of air and water and soil and the irretrievable loss of plant and animal species.

Because of the surging force of such tides of oppression and the great throngs willing—for a time—to ride their wavecrests, such expressions of human freedom turned murderous also precipitate questions about divine "control." In fact, for some they raise another kind of question about "powers" in the world which needs to be considered, in a "parenthesis," here.

(Another Parenthesis:) The Question of a "Satan" Competing for "Control"

Talk about "Satan," or "the Devil," surfaces in times when we discern a mystifying disproportion between a cause rooted in free human actions and an effect overwhelming in its devastation. Did the

Devil bring about the Holocaust? people ask. Does "Satan" enter into certain groups (like the demons invading the swine, in the Mark chapter 5 exorcism story[14]), fomenting movements in which (in the words of the poet Yeats) while "the best lack all conviction, . . . the worst are full of passionate intensity"?

The first answer has to be "no"—but a carefully qualified no.

Everything said earlier about the place of metaphor and symbol in our thinking and speaking—and in the Bible—has to be brought to mind here. If by "devil," or "Satan," we mean a separable spiritual entity, an "intermediate being," in a one-to-one contest with God, then the answer has to be, emphatically, "no." Such a belief radically misrepresents the relation between God and the orders of creation. God the creator and provider does not "share" power with an evil force over against the divine reality.

On the other hand, the symbol "Satan" has to be something more than a misguided "way of talking about" psychological states, mere neurotic or psychotic conditions in individual human beings.

New Testament scholar Walter Wink has addressed this question most helpfully, in a series of studies of what he calls "the powers."[15] Every created thing, Wink suggests—from his work in biblical literatures and in contemporary psychology and social psychology—consists of both an "outer" material reality and an "inner" spiritual reality. But nothing exists without *both* these dimensions and their constant interaction. There are no separable "angels" or "demons" or "gods," but each created entity has its invisible, interior "angel."

It is in the prompting of this "angelic" component that God is at work to provide a "vocation," so to speak, for that particular being and to lure it toward its fulfillment. And what is true of individual creatures is the case also for families, corporations, institutions, or nations. The discernible, though hidden, character of the company one works for, or the country of which one is a citizen, or the political system one espouses—says Wink—can be understood to be its "angel."

But the offices of any such "angel" can be thwarted or misdirected, resulting in a "sick" expression of the originally authentic inner-spiritual reality. If that corrupted version becomes dominant, then what we have been speaking of as "angelic" could better be characterized as "demonic." That is, the energies formerly expended for the fulfillment of a being's "vocation" have now become destructive energies, disintegrative of the self and murderous toward others.

"Satan," then, would be the symbol for the imagined totality of all such demonic compulsions. "Imagined," because this ultimate coming together could never actually take place. But necessary symbol, as well, because without such a naming of this "symbolic repository of the entire complex of evil existing in the present order" (in Wink's phrase)[16] we would be unable to come to terms with even some of the horrors of which we are capable—not God, but we! self-given, as we can be, to the furious fallen angel of our shared human nature—in our collective fear, greed, prejudice and wrath.

Can the question "Is God 'in control'?" be answered: "Yes *and* No?

It must be answered so.

The "no"—this chapter has insisted—is urgently required of us. Why? So that we as believers will be realistic about the world. So that we may not give way to childish dependence on God as cosmic magician. And so that we may learn to be hopeful in God, not merely "optimistic" about what we take to be our chances.

And the "yes"? For those who believe in God as creator and provider, we simply *are* creatures of God, upheld in being by the divine power which is love. Our very existence is a saying "yes" to God.

Any "control" exercised by God has to be a control exercised *in relationship*, and therefore with faithfulness to the terms of that relationship. And what are those terms? Freedom of choice in human creatures and elements of chance in the rest of creation, in unbroken connection with God's irremovable freedom to *be God*, not in glorious divine isolation but as God-*with-us*.

Much of what God can do to "control" the suffering sustained by the creatures of earth is done, therefore, in and through those earth-creatures endowed with an opposable thumb, the capacity to walk on two legs, the gift of language (and of laughter), and the joy and burden of conscious reflection, imagination, and thought.

God's "Control" Exercised through Us in Our Confrontations with Suffering

What is it in our creaturely existence on earth that opens us to suffering, to "the thousand natural shocks" (in Hamlet's words) "that flesh is heir to"? Old, old words come to mind. Famine. Pestilence. Tempest. War.

And what is God "doing" about these horrors—the television images of famine: bodies that are skeletons covered in parchment, emaciated children past weeping; or the statistics on AIDS in Africa, the numbers that outrun our imagination and numb our capacity for feeling; or reports telling of the suffering rampaging weather can visit on us; or the stories featuring violence, with machetes in the jungle, or assault rifles in school-grounds and "improvised explosive devices" by the side of the road, or beatings and sexual abuse in homes—what is God doing? people ask. Is God "in control"?

The answer—one part of an answer, at least—is that God is doing a great deal about it; and *we* are a good part of what is being done: we who are co-creators with God, helping in the *prevention* of the suffering that comes by way of famine, pestilence, tempest, or war.

The centuries have seen remarkable advances in our capabilities for growing, and preserving, and storing food. We can recall, as well, the odyssey of modern medicine, the remarkable burgeoning of medical research and technology of which so many are beneficiaries. Even weather is no longer the thing everybody talks about but nobody can do anything about. If weather patterns can't be altered by our scientists and technicians, they can be anticipated, so that appropriate preparations can be made.

We must not forget those, either, who help in the prevention of suffering through their wise *reflection* on the nature and destiny of humankind, on the causes of violence and war and the conditions making possible a peaceable life together; those who contribute to the training all of us must undergo to become the human beings we are created to be.

But what is God doing, we have also to ask, about the suffering that continues to occur despite all that can be done to prevent it? Again the question turns back on the questioner: What have *we* done, what are we doing, as co-providers with God for the creation, to alleviate the misery attendant on such "natural evils" or deliberate atrocities?

We supply, as we say, *relief*. As to our participation in the divine work of ministering to those who suffer, this is probably the thing we do best and most readily. But co-providers are also co-sufferers, and thus avenues for consolation—"*compassion*" meaning, at root, "suffering together with." How essential is the ministering of those who "weep with those who weep," those who sit with the newly bereaved, or visit with lonely, aged nursing home residents, or serve as hospice volunteers with persons nearing the end—and who know when to suggest some of the truths set forth in this chapter and when (far more importantly!) simply to be there, in silence.

For certain forms of suffering, however, something else is required. Mere relief is insufficient, words of consolation fall short, when the misery arises from a situation that could be changed, from social and economic ailments susceptible to diagnosis and remedy. What is asked of us then is words that help clarify the realities, encouragement toward the right kinds of organized resistance and reform, and our actual participation in such efforts. When the suffering derives from injustice, what is asked of us must encompass *solidarity* with the victims of that injustice in their struggle for a better way.

Whenever such relief is made available, whenever such consolation is given, whenever such solidarity is enacted, God's spirit of love is present, both in those who *offer* the help and in the *recipient* of such help as well.

A parable from Matthew chapter 25 brings home this truth. A great final judgment is envisioned, in which the nations are gathered before the "Son of Man." Some are found worthy to "inherit the kingdom," and some are banished. And what is the basis, the criterion, for this judgment? Help provided for those in need. "I was hungry," says the "Son of Man" from the throne, "I was hungry and you gave me food,"

> "I was thirsty and you gave me something to drink, I was a stranger and you welcomed me, I was naked and you gave me clothing, I was sick and you took care of me, I was in prison and you visited me."

But a question remains: The "righteous" ask,

> "Lord, when was it that we saw you hungry and gave you food, or thirsty and gave you something to drink? And when was it that we saw you a stranger and welcomed you, or naked and gave you clothing? And when was it that we saw you sick or in prison and visited you?"

And the astonishing, sobering answer from the "king" is this: "Truly I tell you, just as you did it to one of the least of these who are members of my family you did it to me."[17]

(A Parenthesis: About What Is Wrong with This Picture)

Clearly, things have been left out, in this report—various realities that cast a deeper shadow over an already clouded terrain. For the truth is that even where the resources for preventing or alleviating suffering abound an undue amount of suffering will still be experienced, especially by those most vulnerable.

Why? Because of a deficiency in the will, the will to marshall the needed resources and effectively and honestly dispense the benefits "Blind spots," as well, whereby sympathies are distorted or deflected. Thoughtless neglect: too few who actually write the check, or make the visit, or prepare the meal. Too few willing to dedicate their gifts, as doctors or nurses or clergy or community organizers or technical specialists, to the needs of those battered by nature's unpredictable energy-bursts or humankind's all-too-predictable violent or covert aggression.

If there is, then, a relationship of mutual love between Creator and creature, wherein "control" is exercised persuasively, never coercively, there is much suffering—we can dare to say, using language we sometimes hear in talk about God and the world's wrongs—that cannot be "blamed on" God. A religious cartoon very much to the point shows two men in conversation. One says, "Sometimes I just want to ask God, when are you going to do something about poverty and child abuse and AIDS and starving people!"

"Well," says the other, "why *don't* you just ask?"

"I'm afraid," comes the answer, "that God might ask *me* the same thing!"

God's "Control" Exercised in Us through our *Receiving* of God's Suffering Love

God's "control" can be exercised through us, then, as we work to change conditions likely to cause suffering and seek afterwards to assuage the suffering that comes despite all such efforts.

But something more needs also to be said. For, along with the relatedness in God, there is also the divine receptivity. God is not just *communicating to* us and the rest of creation the loving, holy, wise, empowering vision of what could be. God is also *receiving from* us and the rest of creation what is happening in response to the divine initiative. And God is, thereby, *remembering*: What God receives from the creation is being "remembered," taken into the divine life, and in the divine-human interchange made newly available for the refashioning of possibilities.

God's "control," then, is exercised not just in our *doing* with God, before and after calamity, but in our *being* with God, throughout, our receiving moment by moment, in faith and love and hope, what God eternally *is* for us and all creation. In such participation in the very life of God, we can learn to allow God's "control," in the yes-*and*-no terms already set forth, to be the defining reality in our lives, in the suffering we ourselves experience and in what we share of the sufferings of others.

"Yes *and* no," then, to the question: Is God in control? And also "I *don't* mean maybe!"?

Our very existence, it was said earlier, is a saying "yes" to God.

But there is something special about our human way of being. The measure of freedom that is ours means that we choose our existence—or, choose the *"humanness"* of our existence; ours is the task, as Marshal McLuhan once wrote, of "learning a living." We have to *learn*, day by day, year by year, about being loved and learning to love, about valuing ourselves and learning to value others, about being co-creators and co-providers in the world, about negotiating the exhilarating but perilous passages of life, about celebrating what is given us and grieving what we lose.

Our "yes," then, to the question about God's "control"—this "yes" held in tension with the "no" already commented on—is not just a statement about what we believe concerning ourselves and our world. It is, even more, a decision about what we will be in this world, about how our relationship with God will be lived out in a suffering world. Each such decision, offered in the face of the "yes *and* no" the questions addressed in this section demand, is a way of saying, somewhere deep within: I *don't* mean "maybe."

Welcoming God's "Control" in Our Life Practice

The question here is how we are to live out that day-to-day decision for God, both in relation to the "regularities" of the world God is continuously creating and for which God is graciously providing and in relation to the disorderings that precipitate suffering. What this comes down to is a matter of learning to welcome, for ourselves, the various ways already considered whereby God exercises "control."

To the way of *action* already identified,—and the way of *reflection*, as well—must be added the way of *prayer*, prayer as both a quality of existence and a conscious discipline. The larger significance of prayer as a life practice is wonderfully encapsulated in the petitions of the prayer which, according to biblical tradition, Jesus taught his disciples. Its first three clauses especially, for they align us with the larger purposes of God for all creation. "Hallowed be your name," we pray—meaning something like: May everything that God is be welcomed in all creation. "Your kingdom come": May the divine rule—God's "control"—be everywhere furthered. And "Your will be done, on earth as in heaven": In specific decisions, may our intention be to participate in God's work done in God's way.[18]

And, finally, the way of *acceptance*. Particular joys or sadnesses, it has been suggested, could involve our sharing with God in God's creative exhilaration or suffering love. Which is to say that God not only creates and provides; God continues also to be present to all the creation, always according to the kind of presence required. And God, moment by moment (even at our final moment) *receives* all created beings—and all that has been done by them and to them and for them—into God's own eternal life.

From the human side of that transaction, what is ultimately being pointed to here is death—death in its various manifestations. The anguishing loss of other lives with whom our life has been in some way entwined. The "death" of certain of our ventures, or certain sustaining beliefs or hopes. And, what each of us—as a unique, self-aware throbbing in the great web of reality—has finally to contemplate, along with the multiplicity of "dyings" in us and all around us: our own leavetaking. In a sense, almost our whole life—from childhood sobbing over a gerbil gone cold and stiff to the later-life habit of reading the newspaper's obituary section first—is a getting ready for the end.

The last form of spiritual practice to be considered here, then, is one whereby we come to reconcilement with death, with this final *loss* of control. Such a coming to terms calls for a belief—as already set forth—in a God who not only welcomes everything into being but also receives all things into God's own eternal life. For anything that is "completed" within the "perpetual perishing"[19] of the process that is reality—a pulsation of energy, a thought or a sigh, a faded blossom, an exchange of words, an organized task or project—has in a sense "died" out of time. What it has become and, in that new life, continues to become God can make available to all that is still ongoing on this side of Hamlet's "undiscovered bourne from which no traveler returns."

The Christian faith invites us to make this vital belief inclusive as well as personal. We can entrust all our own dead to the goodness of a God ready to receive their flaws and their unfulfillments, and the wrongs done them, along with what was commendable in their persons. And faithful imagination can envision the vast concourse of those who have died outside our ken—including the victims of famine and flood waters and a swallowing-up earth, those massacred or tortured and then executed, the millions who perished miserably in death camps or the "gulag archipelago," those suffering fiery death in cities bombed or, anciently, sacked in brutal wars, the infants and children born too early (or too poor) to be kept alive by medical technology—enveloped at last in the healing grace of an unending love.

For death itself, death as such—over against the death that is outrage, serving ancient resentments or twisted ideologies or power-crazed leaders—must not be seen as life's ultimate insult. To perceive our own death so is to is to yield to evil an overwhelming victory, and to cast ourselves and all the rest of humankind in the role of defeated victim. For if death is the ultimate enemy, there is no victory, ever, for anyone. Under such a final, all-negating illusion, death (in Paul's words) *has* "dominion," and we are all in the dreadful state of those "who all their lives [are] held in slavery by the fear of death."[20]

Death *can* be accepted as part of life—the very last part—and as entrance into life: God's eternal life. We can come to believe that "to [God's] faithful people," in the words of the Anglican Burial Office, "life is changed, not ended."[21] We can hope to be able to say that "yes" in the "now" that turns out to be "the hour of our death," when we find ourselves radically alone with the one we have trusted to be a welcoming, receiving God.

Committing ourselves to those hands—which eternally hold and uphold everything in creation—we can reconcile even the "no" and the "yes" of death in all its manifold forms.

ENDNOTES

[1] Science writers espousing such views include: Edward O. Wilson, in *Consilience: The Unity of Knowledge* (New York: Alfred Knopf, 1998); Richard Dawkins, *The Blind Watchmaker: Why the Evidence of Evolution Reveals a Universe without Design* (New York: Norton, 1987); and Daniel Dennett, *Darwin's Dangerous Idea: Evolution and the Meanings of Life* (New York: Simon and Schuster, 1995).

Responses from a Christian perspective have come from: Huston Smith,*Why Religion Matters: The Fate of the Human Spirit in an Age of Disbelief* (HarperSanFrancisco, 2001) and Wendell Berry, *Life Is a Miracle: An Essay Against Modern Superstition* (Washington, D.C.: Counterpoint, 2000).

[2] Albert Einstein, *Out of My Later Years* (New York: Philosophical Library, 1950), 26. A careful, balanced statement on science and religion can be found in Ian Barbour, *When Science Meets Religion: Enemies, Strangers, or Partners?* (HarperSanFrancisco, 2000).

[3] Romans 4:17.

[4] In *The Complete Poems of D. H. Lawrence*, ed. Vivian de Sola Pinto and Warren Roberts (Hammondsworth: Penguin Books, 1964), 690-91.

[5] References are to Genesis 2:15, 18, 20; 1:26; 2:3.

[6] Erik H. Erikson, *Childhood and Society*, rev. ed. (Harmondsworth, Middlesex, England: Penguin Books, 1965).

[7] Genesis 1:1-3.

[8]*The Collected Poems of Dylan Thomas* (New York: New Directions, 1957), 179.

[9] Genesis 3:19.

[10] Mary Oliver, *American Primitive* (Boston: Little, Brown, and Co., 1983), 83.

[11] Terence E. Fretheim, "The God Who Acts: An Old Testament Perspective" (*Theology Today*, 54, no. 1 (April, 1997), 13.

[12] James William McClendon, Jr. *Systematic Theology: Doctrine, Vol. II* (Nashville: Abingdon Press, 1994), 186.

[13] Dan Wakefield, *Expect a Miracle: The Miraculous Things that Happen to Ordinary People* (HarperSanFrancisco, 1995).

[14] Mark 5:1-13; Luke 8:26-33.

[15] Walter Wink, *Naming the Powers: The Language of Power in the New Testament* (Philadelphia: Fortress Press, 1984); *Unmasking the Powers: The Invisible Forces that Determine Human Existence* (Minneapolis: Fortress Press, 1986); *Engaging the Powers: Discernment and Resistance in a World of Domination* (Minneapolis: Fortress Press, 1992).

[16] Wink, *Unmasking*, 24.

[17] Matthew 25:31-40.

[18] Matthew 6:9-10; third clause not present in some texts of the other version, Luke 11:2-3.

[19] Alfred North Whitehead, *Process and Reality : An Essay in Cosmology* (New York: Macmillan, 1929), 517.

[20] Romans 6:9; Hebrews 2:14-15.

[21] *The Book of Common Prayer* (New York: Church Publishing Incorporated, 1979), 382.

CHAPTER FOUR

Is God Our King? Is God Our Father? Our Judge? Our Friend? And other questions about God as covenant partner

"God means," declares Jewish theologian Abraham Heschel: "No one is ever alone."[1] God is not only *present to* us—Heschel would be saying—as self-revealing mystery imparting ultimate meaning to our world. And not only *"ahead of"* us and *for* us as the benign energy creating and providing for the world. This same God is *with* us as well, as our companion in the way, as our "covenant partner."

"No one is ever alone." To many, these words come as an ever-flowing fountain of assurance. For this faith can help assuage the inescapable loneliness of human existence, It can also strengthen the heart in times of anxiety and suffering. "Fear not, I am with thee," Christian worshipers sing (in a hymn paraphrasing promises from Isaiah chapter 43),

> "Fear not, I am with thee; O be not dismayed!
> For I am thy God, and will still give thee aid;
> I'll strengthen thee, help thee, and cause thee to stand,
> upheld by my righteous, omnipotent hand."[2]

For others, however, such insistence on God's nearness may seem anything but reassuring. Is not God our king and also, as such, our judge? Doesn't divine presence entail, as well, divine surveillance, a God on the prowl, searching hearts to discern impulses contrary to the divine will, registering sinful behavior, rendering verdicts, and assigning penalties?

Does it help to say that the God always with us can be thought of as "father," rather than "king" who is also "judge"? What of those for whom the inescapably masculine bias of "father"—especially if coupled with the metaphor of "king"—has to be problematic? All the more when—in teaching regarding God as trinity—Jesus is identified as the "Son" and referred to, accordingly, in nothing but masculine nouns and pronouns and imagery. There has to be something in theologian Mary Daly's challenge: "If God is male, the male is god."[3]

All the same, we cannot settle, either, for the "coziness" of much of the God-as-friend talk so prevalent in our time. We must find also in this God who is our companion on the way the glory and authority associated with the ancient image of kingship, the tenderness combined with wisdom we sense in the "father" invoked by Jesus, and the ideal of holiness and justice seen darkly in the metaphor-mirror of God as judge.

There has to be a way by which we who seek to know the God self-revealed in Holy Scripture can say "yes *and* no" to these perplexing images and yet respond as well with a "yes and I *don't* mean maybe!" to its consistent invitation to know God as covenant partner.

Questions taken up in this chapter, then, include the following:

- Is God a "person"?
- Is God *three* "persons"?
- What is meant by the metaphor of "covenant"? How does covenant entail partnership?
- What is expected of us as God's covenant partners?
- As for *God's* role, what problems are entailed in envisaging the relationship as between:
  —king and subject?
  —father and child?
  —judge and defendant?
  —comrades? friends?
- Can we say both "yes" *and* "no" to these models or metaphors, and at the same time insist that we "*don't* mean maybe!" about the covenant partnership itself?

A preliminary question: Is God a "Person"?

"Father," "king," "judge"—these are images drawn from experiences of personal relationship. Does this mean that we should think of God as a "person"? The answer is yes—if it is kept in mind that this is a provisional yes, with a qualifying no to follow.

We have to answer "yes" because *we* are persons, and our most significant relationships are those in which we as persons engage, oppose, ask help from, or show affection toward other persons. Also because the God of the Bible is presented as acting the way we know persons to act. This God "speaks," acts, calls, intervenes, entreats, shows outrage, appreciation, tenderness.

On the other hand, this is not a one-person show; it's not mime and monologue. Apparently it is of the very essence of the biblical God always to have a dialogue partner. Even at creation, the God who speaks humankind *into* being ("Let us make humankind in our image, according to our likeness") also speaks *to* the humans thus brought into existence. "Be fruitful and multiply, and fill the earth and subdue it."[4] A God who is "the presence to which all reality is present" would have to be present to a *personal* reality in something like a personal way.

Even a cursory look-through reveals the Bible to be one extended interchange between God and a large cast of characters considered to be "people of God." In the Old Testament alone, conversation partners include primordial beings like Adam and Eve, Cain, and Noah; Abraham, that faithful "father of many nations"; Israel's great liberator and lawgiver Moses; Hannah; the prophets—Elijah, Jeremiah, Ezekiel, and numerous others—as well as purely fictional creations like Jonah and (most of all!) Job.

Always these confrontations have to do not just with what God supposedly has to say but also, and especially, with what God is doing. For the Bible makes God known as "personal" even more in terms of deeds than by way of divinely communicated speech. In fact, the words attributed to God, more often than not *are* seen to be deeds: speech-actions by which the contours of cosmic reality are reconfigured.

All that has been said so far about God as "person" is highlighted in the person and career of Jesus of Nazareth, when that life and death are taken to be human manifestations of the divine presence. For the Jesus of the Gospels was himself in close relationship with all the persons who came to receive from him healing grace and transformative teaching, as well as to argue, complain, and reject. And Jesus knew himself to be, at the same time, in intimate fellowship with the one he called Father.

God *can* be spoken of, then, as personal—over against us and in relationship with us, at work in us and for us but also *with* us. To know God is not just to sense that we have "tapped into" some "Force" which is the energy of the cosmos. It is to be in touch with a reality that is beyond our knowing but that engages us, nevertheless, in a mode of relationship like that between persons.

At the same time, the answer also has to be "No." No, God is *not* "a person." The meaning of "God" is irreparably diminished if we think of the divine reality as an entity simply separate from us, as one being among the multitude of other beings. We are participating *in* the divine life—grounded in it, upheld by it, sharing in its creative energy—as well as standing *over against* the divine reality in some of its dimensions.

God *is* a "force," an "energy." And God's relationality extends beyond the human connection: we have to think of the "God of Abraham, Isaac, and Jacob" and "of our Lord Jesus Christ"[5] as the God also of the California redwood, and the crocodile (the monster "Leviathan," in Job), of hummingbirds and bleeding heart, of earthworms and starfish—not to mention amoebas and mitochondria: all the "luminous web" (Barbara Brown Taylor's words) of creation.

Better, then, not to speak of God as "*a* person," but to acknowledge, instead, a dimension in God's being whereby that which is personal in us is being divinely addressed, embraced, fostered, and transformed.

(A Brief Parenthesis): God as **Three** *"Persons"?*

To refer to God, even misleadingly, as "a person" is to bring to mind, for some, the doctrine of the Trinity, whereby God is affirmed as, somehow, both one and three. That's because the "threeness" has traditionally been spoken of by way of the term "persons." "God in three persons, blessed Trinity," we sing. We speak of "God the Father" as the "First Person" of the Trinity, of God the "Son" who was present in the human person Jesus as the "Second Person," and of a "Holy Spirit," active within the divine society-of-three and carrying out the task of being all that God is in and for and with the world.

Quite early in their experience as the Church, Christians realized they knew God in this "threefold cadence," as theologian Elizabeth Johnson puts it, as "beyond them, with them, and within them." But, as she goes on to explain—standing with numerous other twentieth-century theologians who have made this same point—the use of the word "person" to designate the threefold "mystery of distinction . . . at the heart of God" is (in some respects) an unfortunate accident of history. Why? Because what "person" meant for those trying to formulate Christian belief in the earlier centuries of our era differed so greatly from what it has since come to mean. Given the modern understanding of "person" as a separate center of consciousness and volition, "God in three persons" would almost certainly mean "three gods." And because, as well, the traditional designations "Father" and "Son" have led many to envisage at least two of these "persons" as male.

What those long-ago thinkers were trying to affirm by way of the metaphor "person"—and what we continue to affirm as we say the creed they wrote but seek our own understanding of its terms—is the relationality at the heart of what God is. God is one but not solitary. God is love, and that love is interchange, taking place within the divine reality itself (among the "three") as well as flowing out from itself into all creation.[6]

How does the biblical witness picture the relationship between a "personal" God and us?

The divine companionship is implied from the very beginning of the biblical story—in the creation stories of Genesis chapters 1 and 2, the account of the "fall" in chapter 3, and chapter 4's story of the first murder.

The "person"-to-person relationship is even more prominent in the next narrative, that of the Flood. For here, as Noah, his family, and the representatives of other orders of creation disembark on the "mountains of Ararat," God is seen to enter into an agreement with Noah and all those to come after him.[7] According to Scripture, this is the kind of formal agreement called a "covenant." Another, and somewhat different, covenant is made with Abraham, and reconfirmed with Abraham's son Isaac and with Jacob the son of Isaac.[8]

But it is in the second book, Exodus, that the theme of covenant comes to its classic expression. Here, through the prophet-leader Moses and during a protracted pause in the long journey from Egypt, the covenant is established with a whole people: Israel—those considered to be the descendants and heirs of the patriarchs of Genesis.

In the biblical "remembering" of the history of this people, the covenant relationship remains central. From time to time the terms are modified. We are told that, with the advent of monarchy (around the year 1000 BCE), a specific covenant is incorporated into the encompassing agreement. God makes "an everlasting covenant" with David the king and all the successors in this dynasty.[9] The hope for a "messiah" (an "anointed one") eventually to rule Israel and all the world is thought to have derived from the "everlastingness" in this divine promise.

The original covenant was understood to be very much about a promised *land*. But in later centuries terrible things happened that called this promise radically into question. There was an exile (of the people of Judah), a return of sorts from that exile in Babylonia, and a kind of restoration, beginning late in the sixth century BCE. But many people elected to stay in Babylonia, and numerous others had now made their way to other regions of the Middle East. Could the covenant remain in force for these "scattered" ones no longer resident in the land so central to its terms?

Jeremiah and Ezekiel, writing during the time of exile, spoke of an emerging "new covenant." In the covenant to be made "after those days"—says Jeremiah's God—"I will put my law within them, and I will write it on their hearts; and I will be their God, and they shall be my people."[10]

Centuries later, much was made of these renegotiated terms by the members of a Jewish sect following their prophet-and-savior Jesus, as well as by the reconstituted Judaism emerging after the destruction of Jerusalem's Temple in 70 CE.

But the focus now needs to be on the questions overarching all these developments: In light of what we read in Holy Scripture, what was, and what is, a "covenant"? What is it supposed to signify and make possible? What would be entailed in the maintaining of a covenant between God and humankind

The Covenant Partnership:
"I will be their God, and they shall be my people."

The covenant relationship emanates from what God *is* in relation to the world, and provides the means for what God is *doing* in the world. God prepares the covenant terms—the shapers of the biblical story-world would have us understand—presents those terms to the human participants, and (so to speak) "signs" the document.[11]

What is at stake for the covenant-making God of the Bible is the welfare of God's own creatures. For the terms God offers derive from the love and justice understood to be at the heart of the divine reality. Everything God can be for the world is to be made available to all creatures, so that everything particular created beings are capable of becoming can be made available for the good of creation at large.

This is a partnership, therefore. The possibility of divine companionship, guidance, creative challenge, forgiveness, and eternal life is opened by divine grace; it is there for us because of God's goodness. But the making real of these possibilities depends on a loving response, in freedom, from us. "If you obey my voice and keep my covenant," God is heard to say (in Exodus chapter 19), "you shall be . . . for me a priestly kingdom and a holy nation."[12]

Those summoned to faith in Jesus through the preaching of the earliest apostles are appealed to as the "descendants of the prophets and of the covenant that God gave to [their] ancestors."[13] And very near the end of the Christian Bible, it is an echo of Jeremiah's covenant formula that is heard in visionary words concerning earth's ultimate fulfillment:

> the home of God is among mortals.
> He will dwell with them as their God;
> they will be his peoples [or, people],
> and God himself will be with them.[14]

How are we to respond to God's invitation to covenant partnership?

If the divine promise is: "I will be your God," what attitudes and actions are required of us who wish to claim the other part of that promise: "You will be my people"? What are the terms, for us, of this divinely-initiated partnership?

First (and last)—as we have already seen—faith. Faith is our saying "yes" to what God offers us, even if this "yes" incorporates "yes-*and*-no" responses to certain questions of specific belief.

Conscious faith issues in *observance.* As Christians have learned from the antecedent covenant people, persons trying to live by faith in God as covenant partner carry out certain practices derived from the remembered actions of others upholding that way. This is to help us keep central in our thought and practice the first of the two "great commandments," the one about loving "the LORD [our] God with all [our] heart, and with all [our] soul, and with all [our] might."[15]

Among observant covenant partners the notes of *thanksgiving* and *praise*—both in spoken words and in song—will be often sounded. Those under the impression that religious people go about with mostly downturned mouths and sour faces need to recall words spoken by Nehemiah and Ezra to the Jews returned from exile and to all believers after them: "Do not be grieved, for the joy of the LORD is your strength."[16]

Prayer and *meditation* are other means by which the promises of the covenant are claimed and find fulfillment. Walking by faith means learning to embrace silence and to create times of sabbath rest, so that the presence of God can make itself felt.

It also means learning to voice our *complaints* before God. As theologian and philosopher Paul Ricoeur reminds us, the "relationship of the covenant . . . invites us to [articulate] a 'theology of protest.'"[17] There is precedent—in the book of Job, the Psalms of "lament," and in the lives of many we call "saints"—for questioning even the very terms of the covenant and the faithfulness of the divine partner.

Listening for a word from God is essential, also. Through hearing the stories and sayings of Holy Scripture and reflecting on their meaning, we come to know more of what our walk with God can be—and come to a greater acceptance of the mysteries we will never fully comprehend.

For Christian believers, all these observances—praise, thanksgiving, prayer, meditation, listening, and reflecting—center on *Jesus*. For in the life of the earthly Jesus, as witnessed to in Holy Scripture, we find the covenant partnership best exemplified. And through the life of the crucified-and-risen Jesus—offered us in God's Spirit now—we find that covenant most vividly and powerfully there for our receiving.

Covenant faith is also to be expressed in *right action*. To be God's people is to work *with* God in bringing all creation to its fullness in glory. The second of the two "great commandments" speaks emphatically to this calling. "You shall love your neighbor," this one declares—resonating for Christians with the voice of Jesus discerned in the gospel sayings of the New Testament—"you shall love your neighbor as yourself."[18]

One aspect of this moral/ethical dimension of the covenant relationship has to do with the self, the self as (so to speak) our nearest "neighbor." The Bible, and traditional Christian teachings derived from interpretations of the sacred texts, have much to say about individual behavior appropriate to a faithful walk with God.

Some of the commonest misreadings of the Christian way can be traced to an unbalanced emphasis, at certain points in our history, on personal morality. At the same time, some of the commonest distortions of what it means to be a Christian can be seen in the lives of those who claim to be believers but too easily dismiss the teachings of the Bible with regard to the fostering of virtues like single-mindedness, self-control, and moral courage. A cartoon in *Punch* many years ago shows two military persons at the bar in the officers' club contemplating another officer, obviously silly-drunk, whom we recognize as a chaplain. "I'm getting tired," says one officer to his drinking companion, "of his unholier-than-thou attitude."

But most of what Holy Scripture and the Christian ethical tradition have to say about right behavior concerns relationships. Negatively, the point is to avoid actions that can inflict harm—by slanderous speech, or dishonest dealings, or domineering ways, or outright abuse. Positively, what is expected in those committed to the life that is ours in the risen Jesus is what Scripture calls "works of love."

Accordingly, the Jesus presented in the Gospel according to Mark admonishes his disciples that, whereas those recognized as rulers in the world around them "lord it over" the others for whom they are responsible, "it is not so among you; but whoever wishes to become great among you must be your servant, and whoever wishes to be first among you must be slave of all."[19]

A contemporary hymn out of Africa reminds us that

> Neighbors are rich and poor,
> neighbors are black and white,
> neighbors are nearby and far away,

and voices a prayer for a heartfelt response to such need:

> Jesu, Jesu, fill us with your love,
> show us how to serve
> the neighbors we have from you.[20]

Anyone praying such a prayer, however, has to stay open, as well, to *changing* answers to the question "Who is my neighbor?" Jesus expanded some of those answers by his attitudes toward women and children, the poor, and others treated as outcasts in his society. The early church broadened the scope further, admitting into their fellowship the persons called "gentiles" who had been inadmissible by the terms of the covenant with Israel. Later centuries have seen further inclusions—of people of color, women, persons of homosexual orientation—which have further altered earlier boundaries.

How often, though, we do wrong by our divine covenant partner and the fellow earth-dwellers we are to love as ourselves. We allow our faith to grow weak through lack of observance. We misrepresent the God known to us in Jesus by our personal lack of moderation, humility, and consistency, as well as our paltry, grudging efforts to serve our near-at-hand or far-away "neighbors."

What, then? Then we are called, according to biblical teaching, to *penitence*. In our walk with God—as well as in our most intimate relationships with fellow human beings—the truth we require to hear, it could be said (in direct contradiction of a famous saying from a famous 'sixties novel made into a film), is this: "Love means *always* having to say you're sorry."

This walk with God, finally, needs to be a dimension of *all our experience*, whether of self, or other persons, or the world around us. Accordingly, for any of us "whose hearts are set on the pilgrims' way,"[21] God's companionable presence graces our inmost feelings, intuitions, and ideas; our silences and our dream-time and our solitary walks; our dealings with other persons with whom we work, play, talk, make love; our many routine actions, as well as our "observant" times of serious reflection, or prayer, or worship.

What are we to do with the biblical images, or models, of this covenant partnership?

Anything we are able to say about the relationship between God and us—let the indispensable truth be stated again!—has to be expressed in metaphor and story. And so the scriptural witness to humankind's journeyings with God identifies God in various contexts as our "king," our "father," our "judge," even (especially in the person of Jesus as embodying divine presence) our "friend."

What has to be considered now is whether we can respond to such imagery with both a "yes" and a "no" while yet affirming truths that come to us thereby with a strong "yes and I *don't* mean maybe!"

"Yes and *No" to God as "King"*

Again and again in the Bible God is spoken of, or addressed, as "king." "The LORD is king forever and ever." God is "a great King above all gods." The one the prophet Jeremiah serves is "the living God and the everlasting King."[22] The Jesus whose cross carried the mocking superscription "King of the Jews" is exalted in other late-first-century writings (the words echo in our minds from Handel's "Hallelujah Chorus") as "King of kings and Lord of lords."[23]

Surely, though, we have to say "no" to such a model for covenant partnership. To begin with, monarchy is simply not part of our experience—or it figures only as an almost empty shell of its former splendor and import.

Even more to the point, would not such an image of sovereignty, if it could be taken seriously, loom as a threat to human freedom? For the monarchs of ancient days were, more often than not, absolute rulers, holding the power of life and death over their subjects, often keeping them under surveillance by way of an intricate network of spies.

The king's subjects were expected to learn attitudes of submission and gestures of servility: using special titles like "your majesty," "bowing and scraping," presenting petitions rather than entering into dialogue or conversation. (One recalls the moment, in that bracingly irreverent film *Monty Python and the Holy Grail*, when a god-like voice is heard giving contrary advice, from out of a highly-ornamented cloud: "Don't grovel!")

The *language* of kingship, finally, reflects the male bias affecting not only the actual leadership of the church's worship and its common life but also, even more subtly, the language of that worship and of the Holy Book at its center. The pronouns are almost invariably "he" and "his"; nouns like "king," "lord," "master" carry masculine connotations: metaphors of warriorship, law-making, and control of property and people are associated with stereotypically masculine pursuits.

But a "yes" is also possible to the traditional understanding of God as king. At the very least, we can modify some of the terms of the "no" already suggested. For the biblical model of kingship is not that of absolute, arbitrary rule. It is, so to speak, "constitutional," to be carried out according to principles understood to derive from the divine nature. Since the covenant was in force for kings as well as for their subjects, Israel's prophetic spokespersons could call royal arrogance and tyranny to account. God as king, therefore, in covenant relationship with us as subjects, will reign as "good shepherd" (to use a favorite metaphor of the prophet Ezekiel[24]) rather than the impersonal, arbitrary, domineering presence our imaginations are prone to project.

Central to Jesus' teaching was the nearness of what he called the "kingdom of God." In its content, however, this teaching was mainly an attempt to provide some sense of what the *relationship* can be like—including such elements as mercy, a spirit of forgiveness, reckless generosity, attentiveness to the sick, the poor and the oppressed, single-hearted commitment to the cause of righteousness, and (the summing-up characteristic) unfailing love—between God as ruler and the people giving covenant allegiance.

After his death, the Jesus who had preached the rule of God came to be preached, himself, as the fulfillment of that hope. And Christ as king was remembered not only as acting to assuage the sufferings of the people but as entering into the sufferings themselves—on a cross!—in the self-giving vulnerability of divine love. If the image of God as king can still serve, it would be an image including such vulnerability and self-emptying that we would have to uphold.

At the same time, should not such an image serve also to recall to our minds from ancient days royal splendor and magnificence? The natural world which is God's creation "*is* charged," as the poet reminds us, "with the grandeur of God." And so is humankind at its best. From both these realms shines forth the glory of their creator.

For glory is the issue here. And authority. To convey some sense of the fullness of divine glory glimpsed in the world around us we may need to retain some, at least, of the ancient symbolism of kingship still available to our cultural memory, and thus counter the presumptuous coziness of too many imaginings of God as "friend."

"Yes **and** *No" to God as "Judge"*

In ancient monarchies, kings would also often be judges, dealing with at least certain cases that might be brought before them. With regard to the biblical understanding of God, there was no question: God the king was also God the judge, both as law-*giver*, providing the directives known as the Ten Commandments and the whole "package" spoken of as the "book of the covenant"[25] and also taking ultimate responsibility for *enforcing* these laws and administering penalties for violations.

In the New Testament, the person of Jesus—and, later, the risen Christ—comes to be associated with law itself and judgment more generally. People subscribing to the "gentle Jesus meek and mild" image can be shocked at how often the sayings and stories ascribed to Jesus in the gospels sound the note of judgment. A manager, for example (in one of the parables in Luke), who has been abusing the workers and neglecting his own responsibilities really "gets it" when the owner comes on the scene.[26]

For Paul the apostle, what is revealed in Scripture and in human experience is not only the graciousness of a loving God but the "wrath" of a just God. And the author of Hebrews warns (in words made famous through a sermon of the eighteenth-century divine Jonathan Edwards) that "it is a fearful thing to fall into the hands of the living God."[27]

Because this metaphor so often goes awry, many are more than ready to say "no" to God as judge. Even the most helpful laws, for one thing, can be wrenched to fit the selfish interests of certain persons holding power, thus furthering oppression rather than merely maintaining peace and order.

Our understanding of God as judging *us* can go damagingly out of balance when we automatically ascribe painful circumstances to divine punishment rather than taking account, as well, of human free choice and of elements of randomness in the natural order. I remember an eighty-year-old woman newly resident in a nursing home whose complaint always took this form: "I don't know why God is doing this to me!"

This is a danger especially if God is envisioned as a king, or old-style father, wielding absolute power. As the Santa Claus, we could even say, of the Christmas ditty:

> You better watch out,
> better not cry,
> better not pout,
> I'm telling you why:
> Santa Claus is comin' to town! . . .
>
> He sees you when you're sleepin',
> he knows when you're awake,
> He knows if you've been bad or good,
> So be good, for goodness' sake!
> Oh, you better watch out, etc.[28]

Our "yes" to an aspect of the covenant relationship in which God is understood to be our judge can be affirmed only if certain truths are kept in mind. First, that the limits or rules with respect to which we incur judgment are a divine gift, a part of God's merciful provision for the world—since without such guidelines both individual existence and social arrangements would fall into destructive disorder. Second, that God's judgment is not to be thought of as quasi-personal divine "wrath" but as the inevitable consequence of a perverse, though freely rendered, decision on our part. And—last, but most important—that divine grace is always prior to judgment. The guilt we feel about acts of cold indifference or willful cruelty derives from our sense of having blocked currents of divine love already flowing.

"Yes and *No" to God as "Father"*

Among all the ways Christian tradition refers to our connection with God, the image of God as our father is predominant. Only in our time has there been heard any sort of firm "no" to that metaphor.

Some of the terms of that opposition have already been set out. The male bias in the language, for one thing: the prevalence of "father" / "son" / "he," and "his." The tendency as well to carry such top-down relationships into the ordering of human relations. The "man of the house," then, is the "king" in his "castle," and both the woman and the children of that house are subject to his authority and rule. "He for God only," the great 17th-century poet John Milton writes (in *Paradise Lost*) concerning the one taken to be our ultimate ancestor, Adam; "she"—his consort Eve—"for God in him."[29]

Such an image of family life clashes with the hard-learned wisdom of recent times. Furthermore, when it is applied, one-sidedly, to our covenant relationship with God, it can lead to an unhealthy dependency and/or fear. Love, in these terms, is not mutual love; God condescends to care for us. Our love, in turn, will tend to be slavish and clinging: "'Daddy' will take care of me." "I mustn't complain: Father knows best."

But a "yes" at once clamors to be heard. For one thing, the God worshiped by Christian believers is "the God and Father of our Lord Jesus Christ." But Jesus' "Father"-language reflects the nature of that *relationship*; it has nothing to do with gender. The qualities perceived in the person of Jesus, as witnessed to in the Gospels, vouch for the envisioned qualities, also, of his father (and mother) God.

Such a fatherhood, furthermore, means that all human beings are brothers and sisters. This truth, as well, was exemplified in the life of

Jesus of Nazareth, in his welcoming of all who came to him in need and in his dealings with those being prepared by him for a more extensive mission.

"Yes and *No" to Other Images for our Covenant Partnership with God*

Can we say that God is our "friend"? Our "mother"? Our "lover"? There is warrant for all these metaphors—and others as well—in Scripture and in the church's tradition.

Abraham was a friend of God. About to destroy Sodom and Gomorrah, God makes the divine intention known to Abraham, saying: "Shall I hide from Abraham what I am about to do . . .?" The great leader Moses is described as one "whom the Lord knew face to face."[30]

Near the end of the first century, someone writing the gospel attributed to John remembered (or imagined) Jesus saying to his disciples, as he approached his end, "I do not call you servants any longer, because the servant does not know what the master is doing; but I have called you friends, because I have made known to you everything that I have heard from my Father."[31]

Yes, then, by all means, to the image of God as friend. Yes to opening that possibility not only to "stars" like Abraham or Moses but to ordinary folk like Jesus' disciples—and to us who seek to follow Jesus in our own day.

Yes, as well, to the image of God as mother, one who begets and bears and nourishes children—the mother of the scene evoked by sociologist Peter Berger cradling the infant who has cried out in the night and murmuring, over and over, "Don't be afraid. Everything is all right."[32]

And yes to God as lover. Not just the jealous husband found in the writings of prophets like Hosea and Jeremiah, passionately angry at the people of Israel in the imagined role of faithless wife, but the lover desiring and cherishing the beloved.

A "no" is called for as well, however—a cautionary "no." In our time especially, such images can render the relationship (as already suggested) too "easy." Nowadays, "conversations with God" that are little more than projections of religious pet peeves and "New Age" "wannabes" can stay on best seller lists for months. The kind of religiosity identified, in Robert Bellah's *Habits of the Heart* as "Sheilaism" flourishes. It consists of beliefs associated with no faith tradition but formulated by an individual, beliefs like those of the interviewee in the Bellah study named Sheila: "It's just try to love yourself and be gentle with yourself. You know, I guess, take care of each other. I think He would want us to take care of each other."[33]

"Yes *and* no" to such metaphors and, also, "I *don't* mean maybe!" to God's covenant?

Such a "yes-*and*-no" response to the images presented can help clear the way for a free, open, balanced "yes" to the invitation to be God's covenant partners.

And so we dare a "*no*":

No to the idea of God as unapproachable majesty who, at best, "condescends" to care about us.

No to a God conceived as arbitrary, autocratic ("almighty") ruler who "can do anything," even set aside the laws of nature.

No to servile behavior toward God "above"—and toward those claiming to be "above" us as God's earthly representatives.

No to God as "male"—and the exclusive use of masculine language for talk about God.

No to legalistic, rule-dominated, merely dutiful attitudes toward God as judge.

No to interpretations of personal suffering as necessarily a penalty meted out by a judging God.

No to slavish dependence on God as "daddy."

No, as well, however, to understandings of God, old or new, that dim the divine glory, domesticate the fierceness of the divine energy, and discount divine judgment.

For each negation, however, we can also affirm a "yes." We learn to do this as we come more and more to trust the assurances offered by the eternally faithful, loving God we know in Jesus. We learn it as we seek to follow the way of observance, service, and penitence. We learn thereby a "yes *and* no" undergirded by an enduring "and I *don't* mean maybe." And thus we find ourselves more and more able to affirm:

That because God is with us, as "the beyond in the midst," we are "never alone."

That because God is "sovereign," rightly commanding: "You shall have no other gods before me," none of us has to "play god."

That, walking with this lawgiver-God, rejoicing in the grace of divinely-provided limits, we need not consider moral and ethical decisions simply "up for grabs."

That, because divine grace is prior to judgment, we can hope to do right in our choosing and not fall into despair when we have done wrong. We do not have to go the way of this "hellish world," as Alan Jones calls it, "in which everything is permitted, yet nothing is forgiven."[34]

That, with God as our "motherly" father, we can learn to be brothers and sisters one to another as members of the largest family imaginable.

That we can—with Abraham, and Moses, and the disciples of Jesus—be friends with God.

That we can let all experiences and relationships in life be occasions for further imaginative exploration into God. We can, as contemporary hymn writer Brian Wren suggests in one of his compositions, "bring many names"—including (among those he presents) "strong mother God," "warm father God," even "old, aching God" and "young, growing God"—to celebrate the covenant partner whom we worship and love.[35]

ENDNOTES

[1] Abraham Heschel, *Man Is Not Alone* (New York: Farrar, Straus and Young, 1951), 109; cited in Alan Jones, *The Soul's Journey: Exploring the Three Passages of the Spiritual Life with Dante as a Guide* (HarperSanFrancisco, 1995), 212.

[2] From the hymn "How firm a foundation," found in numerous church hymnals, among them *The Hymnal 1982, according to the use of The Episcopal Church* (New York: Church Hymnal Corporation, 1982), hymn 636.

[3] Mary Daly, *Beyond God the Father: Toward a Philosophy of Women's Liberation* (Boston: Beacon Press, 1973), 19.

[4] Genesis 1:28.

[5] Exodus 3:6; 1 Peter 1:3.

[6] Elizabeth A. Johnson, "Trinity: To Let the Symbol Sing Again," *Theology Today* 54, no. 3 (October 1997), 304-305.

[7] Genesis 9:8.

[8] Genesis 15:17-20; 17:1-8.

[9] 2 Samuel 23:5

[10] Jeremiah 31:31-33.

[11] The language about God as "king" reflects, in part, this divine initiative. Some scholars have traced certain aspects of covenant declarations in Holy Scripture to an ancient treaty form whereby a Middle Eastern sovereign in a position of strength would offer to another ruler or to a subject people terms whereby their security would be maintained and the sovereign's interests advanced. See the discussion of covenant in Bernhard W. Anderson, *Understanding the Old Testament*, Fourth Edition (Englewood Cliffs, N.J.: Prentice-Hall, 1986), 98-101.

[12] Exodus 19:5-6.

[13] Acts 3:25.

[14] Revelation 21:3.
[15] Deuteronomy 6:5.
[16] Nehemiah 8:10.
[17] Paul Ricoeur, *Figuring the Sacred: Religion, Narrative, and Imagination*, trans. David Pellauer (Minneapolis: Fortress Press, 1995), 252, 260.
[18] Leviticus 19:18, cf. Matthew 22:37-40; also Paul, in Romans 13:9-10.
[19] Mark 10:42-44.
[20] Ghanian, trans. Thomas S. Colvin, *The Hymnal 1982, according to the use of The Episcopal Church* (New York: Church Hymnal Corporation, 1982), hymn number 602.
[21] Psalm 84:5—version in *The Book of Common Prayer* (New York: Church Publishing Inc., 1979), 707.
[22] Psalm 10:16; 95:3; Jeremiah 10:10.
[23] Revelation 19:16.
[24] Ezekiel 34:4, 10.
[25] Exodus 24:7.
[26] Luke 12:42-48.
[27] Romans 1:16-18; Hebrews 10:31.
[28] Haven Gillespie and J. Fred Couts, "Santa Claus Is Comin' to Town" (London: EMI Music).
[29] John Milton, *Paradise Lost*, Book IV, line 299.
[30] Genesis 18:17ff.; Deuteronomy 34:10.
[31] John 15:15.
[32] See note 11, Chapter One.
[33] Robert Bellah et al., *Habits of the Heart: Individualism and Commitment in American Life* (Berkeley and Los Angeles: University of California Press, 1985), 221.
[34] Jones, *Soul's Journey*, 93.
[35] Brian Wren, *Bring Many Names: Thirty-Five New Hymns by Brian Wren* (Carol Stream, IL: Hope Publishing Co., 1989), hymn no. 9.

CHAPTER FIVE

Does Prayer "Change Things"?
A Further Question about God as Covenant Partner

Why pray? Because we believe—or want to believe—that there is a self-revealing Something "out there" or "in here." Because that beyond-in-the-midst, rightly understood, is "in control" as creator and provider. And because this that we name God can be known as a companioning presence.

We pray, then, our awe and wonder, even if only by an "O God!" detonated by some overpowering manifestation in nature or the human spirit. We pray our gratitude, for divine presence and provision. Knowing ourselves to have fallen short of God's intended glory, we pray our penitence and our desire for restoration and renewal. But most of us, most of all, pray our immediate needs. "God, help me!" is our cry—or, "Help this one I so love!"—and it is torn from us by wrenching pain or heart-stopping dread.

And this is where problems of belief come to nag at us. Why doesn't this father take better care of us the members of the family? Why doesn't this good king do more to ensure the welfare of us creature-subjects? And does prayer, in such perplexity (in the words of a popular religious slogan), does "prayer change things"? If a "no" has to be said to this question, can a "yes" be just as strongly affirmed? Can we follow with a confident "and I *don't* mean maybe!" concerning the faithful *practice* of such prayer?

Specific questions to be touched on in this chapter include the following:

- What does experience tell us about prayer-as-asking?
  Do we always get what we pray for?
  Do we ever get what we pray for?
- What does the Bible advocate with regard to prayer?
- What belief-context can make sense of both ancient and modern attitudes toward prayer, and what model can it provide for prayer-as-asking?

- In this relational model, what do we bring to the situation prompting our prayer? What does God bring to that situation?
- How can prayer, on this model, "change things"—in the situation prayed about? in us doing the praying?
  How is prayer ultimately "answered"?
- How can we say "yes *and* no" to the question about prayer-as-asking, and also learn to affirm a "yes and I *don't* mean maybe!"?

Must we say "No" to the question "Does prayer 'change things'?"

The answer to the question posed in this chapter has to be, in some respects, "No." For many, it is disillusioning experience—prayer *not* "answered"—that impels the negative conclusion. The cancer turned out to be not "all gone." The hoped-for financial rescue did not "pan out." The God prayed to did not avert a meaningless conflict, did not "save."

If we are asking (as in Chapter Three), "Is God 'in control'?" the question raised would take the form: "What kind of world is it where . . .?" Is this a world without God? A world whose God is powerless to "answer" prayers? If the issue concerns (as in Chapter Four) a God with whom we are "covenant partners," then our question might be more like a protest: "What kind of a *God* is it who . . .?" For if it is insisted that there *has* been an answer from that God, it would have to be said that God chose to deny the request.

Harder yet to deal with is the suggestion that it's somehow our fault. We didn't pray "hard enough," or pray "aright." Or we didn't "deserve" a favorable answer. Does the saving action of God depend, then, on our goodness, or our fervency, or some special awareness on our part as to the divine intention?

Some of what is uncritically affirmed about prayer serves not to shore up but to breach certain uninspected belief structures and thus invade the soul with doubts.

> What about this Sunday School lesson, for instance, meant to illustrate God's faithfulness in answering prayer? The members of the class were told to form cookie shapes out of clay, and then put this "cookie dough," on a baking sheet, into an oven in the church kitchen. In a little while, a batch of delicious sugar cookies was taken from the oven, and the children were invited to eat them. The lesson intended? Obviously, that the prayers we offer God can yield wonders analogous to the "miracle" just witnessed. The lesson

learned? More likely, something about phony church people and a God who is equally unreal.

But can the question "Does prayer 'change things'?" also be answered "Yes"?

We can start, here also, with *experience*. With the numerous accounts, for one thing, of remarkable healings associated with prayer. With medical research results indicating the efficacy of faith, as expressed in praying, with respect to good health generally and post-operative recovery of heart patients, more specifically.[1]

There is also the Bible's unfaltering advocacy of prayer. "Far be it from me," declares the prophet and leader Samuel to the ancient people of Israel, "that I should sin against the Lord by ceasing to pray for you." "The prayer of the righteous," the New Testament assures Christian believers, "is powerful and effective."[2]

Jesus taught his followers what came to be called "the Lord's Prayer," and directed them toward a God eager to hear prayers and to give what is asked therein. Numerous glimpses are given of Jesus as himself a person of prayer, frequently going out "to a deserted place" "by himself to pray," crying out to God in anguish, "deeply grieved, even to death," in the place called Gethsemane.

The Acts of the Apostles is suffused with the spirit of prayer and dotted with reconstructed prayers by members of that emerging body the "church." The "letters" sent by the Apostle Paul and other church leaders regularly urge members of Christian assemblies to "persevere in prayer" and even to "pray without ceasing."[3]

But such a "yes" requires, also, a particular *context* of belief. For many a 21st-century skeptic, neither contemporary healing stories nor citations from ancient holy writings carry much weight. Anciently, a considerable range of "wonders" could be ascribed to divine actions—including certain cures—which 21st-century people would want to trace to causes within the system we call "nature." Many today take the Bible's very special "answers to prayer" to be outright inventions put forward to make Jesus and his followers "look good."

God can be understood, however, in a way that incorporates both the "yes" of the Bible's witness and contemporary "wonders" and aspects of the "no" offered by the modern worldview. Such an understanding of God as "creator and provider" and "covenant partner" requires that we conceive of God as relating *"personally"* to what is personal in us, thereby enabling us to voice our joys and griefs and concerns before God the way we open our hearts to one another as human beings.

This radical *relationality* also requires us to take full account of freedom—*all* freedoms: the wise, loving, empowering divine vision of what can be; human freedom to choose among perceived alternatives; and an element of "chance" in the processes of nature as they enter into the workings of human history.

The interplay among these energies—Holy Scripture affirms—is activated by *love*. Whatever God does will be ultimately for the fulfillment, in joy and peace and abundant life, of all creation. And the power by which this work is accomplished will be the strength of God's loving desire, informed by the infinite wisdom that continually envisions ways for the fulfilling of the divine intention.

In such a context, the act of praying is something very different from coming to Dad (or Mom) to ask for an increase in one's allowance or an evening's use of the family car. Different even from petitioning a great king for gifts or favors desired by the subject and simply lying within the power of the monarch to grant. We need to be able to think of prayer in ways other than the one-sided understanding bequeathed by metaphors of divine kingship and (mostly male) parenthood.

How *can* prayer be pictured, then, in such a context? Like this, perhaps: We enter *with* God into a given situation—pain-filled, it may be, or just problematically open and confusing. We seek, with God, to discern possibilities in that situation. We submit our selves to the powerful energy of divine love and wisdom, in order that we may both accept conditions clearly beyond our reach and work patiently, resourcefully, at what is doable. The Serenity Prayer of the "Twelve-step" groups is very much in place here: "God grant me the courage to change what can be changed, the serenity to accept what cannot be changed, and the wisdom to know the difference."

We enter "*with* God" into the situation that impels us to prayer. But what is to be done in that situation, then—by us who pray and by the God to whom we pray? And why would it matter that such prayers are offered? Do those prayers "change things"?

What do *we* bring to the situation concerning which prayer is offered?

To the kind of praying just described, we bring *ourselves*, and whatever is in our feelings and thoughts at the moment of prayer. I was greatly helped in this regard by a well-known churchman who insisted, in a gathering where I was present: Bring everything before God in prayer. Don't restrict yourself to what you consider 'the will of God.' Don't 'censor' your prayers.

We bring *persistence* in asking. Jesus tells a story about a widow whose cause is vindicated by a judge known to be "unjust," simply because she "keeps bothering" him. "Will not God," asks Jesus, seeking to bring home the point of the parable. "grant justice to his chosen ones who cry to him day and night?"[4] Throughout the Bible, God's favorite people are often the "pushiest" ones, the ones—like Abraham, and Moses, and Job (and Jesus! not to mention Paul)—who keep asking, and complaining, until something enters the situation to resolve it.

We bring the network of *personal relations* that is ours. The voicing of our sincere desire for another's welfare becomes part of what God has available to (so to speak) work with. We bring, as well, our *past*—recent and long ago happenings of which we are clearly or dimly aware. We bring (like it or not!) our participation in the regularities and randomnesses of the *"natural" order"*—bodily processes, tectonic plates, weather patterns, chemical interactions. More than that, we bring to the "mix" our own *freedom to act*, to bring about change, in ourselves, in our relationships, and even in some of the circumstances of our lives.

And we bring our *faith*. Not feelings—feelings of optimism, let's say, the sense that "things generally work out for the best." Not mere articles of belief: "I believe that God is all-powerful." Right beliefs can support faith (and inadequate beliefs can undermine it!)—but belief is not the same thing as faith. "In faith," writes Brother David Steindl-Rast, "[we raise our eyes] above the horizon of [our] beliefs."[5]

What does *God* bring to the situation?

Faith as spoken of here has to do simply with how we stand toward God. In what, or in whom, do we ultimately put our trust? From that perspective of belief, however, to come to God in faith is to ask, once again: What can we affirm about God? About God, more specifically, in relation to us and our world?

For what must be insisted on, at the beginning of our thinking and at its end, is that what God brings to the situation lifted up by us in prayer is the divine reality itself. We pray because of God. We pray to God and, in a sense, with God. What we receive, ultimately, as the answer to our prayer is: God.

We receive God as inexhaustible, incomprehensible mystery, a Mystery that is endlessly self-giving, self-revealing. As eternal creativity and caring, the One through whom all is coming into being and through whom all is sustained and provided for. As ultimate wisdom, informing each moment with a sense of the best possibilities for fulfilling the divine vision. As love, nurturing, forgiving, restoring, transforming—always subject to our embrace in freedom of whatever can be seen as furthering God's rule in all things. And as life—eternal life, continually taking into itself all that has been felt and thought and done by God's creatures, in order that it may be judged, healed, and offered in renewed glory to the ongoing creation.

Prayer happens whenever we open ourselves in any way to this divine mystery continually present to us and to our world. Prayer is a conversation between us and God—we are reminded by Brother Martin Smith, SSJE—and it is God who initiates that interchange, not we; prayer, in all its forms, is our response to the divine speaking.[6]

As Christians, we affirm that God enters into the situation in another aspect as well. For in the act of praying we are met by that in the divine reality which was present two thousand years ago in the human reality of Jesus of Nazareth and indwells us now as the Spirit of the ever-living Christ.

To pray "in the name of Jesus" means bringing to mind what Jesus said and did, as witnessed to in the New Testament, retracing in story and sacramental action the end of that life of love and truth—and the life beyond life granted him in that event within God's eternal life that believers call the "resurrection." Affirming, as well, that in this chosen one, this "Christ," God "was reconciling the world to himself."[7]

For in Jesus God was entering, in a new way, into the elements of human existence, including (especially!) human suffering. As a twentieth-century hymn assures us,

> . . . when human hearts are breaking
> under sorrow's iron rod,
> then we find the selfsame aching
> deep within the heart of God.[8]

Praying "in the name of Jesus," we align ourselves with Jesus' trust in the God he called "father," even in experiences of misunderstanding and rejection and in the final extremity. We rest in the hope that all the joys and longings and sufferings expressed in our prayers are known to God in the way they were known to the fully-human Jesus, and that all the healing and fulfillment opened to Jesus through participation in the divine life are open to us as well who know God in Jesus.

God is present to the situation summoning us to prayer in yet a third way: God is there as the Holy Spirit. "We do not know how to pray as we ought," the Apostle Paul writes, "but [the] Spirit intercedes with sighs too deep for words" [or, in the more familiar earlier translation: "with groanings that cannot be uttered"]. This is a very capacious understanding of prayer: prayer as "groaning," or "sighing."

Paul imagines "the whole creation . . . groaning in labor pains until now"; and goes on to suggest that "not only the creation but we ourselves . . . groan inwardly."[9]

We "do not know how to pray as we ought"; and the earth itself groans with us. Could this mean also that God—God the Holy Spirit—shares in that perplexity? Could it be that, though God has an encompassing vision for us and all other creatures, God, too, is groaning in perplexity and (as it were) labor pains with respect to what actually can come to pass in this moment? We don't know the answer. The Spirit of God, then, entering into our praying, doesn't know the answer, either—that is, doesn't "know *the* answer," but can only remain open to the available, or conceivable, possibilities. At that moment, it is not so much that *we* are asking things *from God* as that asking is going on in which we and (somehow) the Spirit of God are both engaged.

How can prayer, so understood, "change things"?

How can prayer so understood *not* change things? But, we must still ask,what kind of change? What degree of change? And in what way connected to the act of praying?

How could prayer change the situation itself?

One answer offered to the question "Does prayer 'change things'?" is: Prayer changes *us*, changes the ones doing the praying. But many won't sit still for such a solution. I'm not praying, someone will say, to become more patient, more submissive to the divine will; I'm praying for God to heal my cancer, to release some beloved person from an addiction or a destructive relationship. I'm bringing before God my own need to be loved, to be valued, to find something to do that will make a difference in the world. What difference could my praying make with regard to predicaments such as these?

Given the intermeshing of freedoms presupposed in the model presented earlier, some of these prayers will not be "answered": the wished-for outcome will not happen. Will not happen, that is, in the terms in which it is wished for. Asking for these things is not wrong. Expecting answers is not wrong. But the *terms* of the expectation—and, in a sense, of the asking—can come to be seen as misguided.

In prayer as understood here, we are not petitioners beseeching God-as-cosmic-magician or God at some celestial control panel to work wonders that overpower human freedom or set aside the "laws of nature." We are, instead, responding with God to a specific situation and seeking, with God—in the intensity of our need and the hard-pressed courage of faith—outcomes that will further the just and loving rule of God. The prayer within our prayer, in other words—ancient, familiar words!—is: "Thy kingdom come; thy will be done, on earth as it is in heaven."

We enter the situation with God. Having entered, we pray to the God who is with us there. And then, we expect answers *from* God. But the answer we are to expect, centrally, is an answer that *is* God: God's loving presence, God's saving work (we being co-creators and co-providers), God's ever-welcoming eternity.

But this presence, this working, this eternal life mean wonders *can* happen! In the situation itself. For in the mystery of divine freedom and human freedom and the "laws" of nature, what is capable of happening is always—in the words of the Letter to the Ephesians—"far more than all we can ask or imagine."[10] A friend's tumor, to the amazement of physicians, diminishes in size and then disappears. A drug-addicted daughter or son, long prayed for, finds release. An oppressive empire collapses from within, with very few shots being fired. "Ah!" we say (under our breath, perhaps!) "Our prayers have been answered."

No one knows exactly how such things come to be—nor why other concerns just as earnestly prayed about are not similarly resolved. But on such occasions things do change. Through prayer by which we seek to join with God in "opening the possibles" (the words are those of Walter Wink)[11] balances shift, patterns reconfigure, energies are blessedly renewed.

How could prayer change **us***?*

Are we to say, though, that God "co-operates for good with those who love God" when prayers are not "answered," when there are no wonders: the sick person stays sick, war continues to ravage a countryside, the cloud of depression does not lift, helpless people groan under ever more grievous injustice?

Yes. We are part of the situation concerning which our prayers have been offered, having entered into it, with God, through our praying. The situation also changes, then, if this interchange contributes to something transformative in *us*. The same can be true with respect to others for whose needs we intercede when they experience a similar soul-change even though the circumstances of their suffering remain in place.

For one thing, we can find ourselves *comforted*—as can they. For we are never alone in our grief. The God present in Jesus is a God who suffers, who shares our distress and confusion. God's own Spirit grieves ("groans"!) with us. And provides means by which we find solace.

Or we can find ourselves *confronted*, confronted with overlooked realities, such as to change even what we pray *for*. We come to realize that what we have been asking is wrong for us—sinfully wrong, if it violates some basic term of our relationship with the one who is a God of holiness as well as of unfailing love.

Or we are startled to learn that the "answer" we had thought would require some "miracle" from "outside" calls instead for immediate common-sense *action* by us or others known to us. We say, "O God, answer my prayer," and we hear: "Answer it yourself: say that timely word, write that letter or email, do some personal heart-searching, get on with those vexing negotiations." "Through prayer," writes theologian Marjorie Suchocki, "we open ourselves to the divine will, so that the guidance fashioned for us in heaven might be felt and effected on earth."[12]

Often the change taking place is simply that we find ourselves empowered to *endure*, by way of a deep-down serenity that "accepts what cannot be changed." Such *acceptance* may be hardest of all. Problem-solving action turns out to be impossible. Negotiations collapse. Nature rampages on. Individuals assert their freedom in opposition to what is clearly the divine vision of what could be. What is left is acceptance—the second part of the prayer torn from Jesus in Gethsemane: after the "If it is possible let this cup pass . . .," the "Not what I want but what you want."[13] It is not fatalistic resignation that is asked for: *Que será, será*. Nor passive submissiveness. Rather, what we have finally to be capable of, after the anguished pleading, after all our efforts, is authentic acceptance, in faith.

Why? Because of God. Ultimately, the Christian faith tells us, the answer to all our prayers is God. Even if the immediate answer we have envisioned doesn't come, the ultimate Answer remains present to us and at work with us. Remains present also to the situation precipitating our prayers, and at work there—continually—despite all the resistances and rejections.

How do we say "yes *and* no" to the question about prayer and also "I *don't* mean maybe!"?

In the face of the required "yes *and* no" to the question "Does prayer 'change things'?" we can nevertheless struggle toward a confident "And I *don't* mean maybe!" One thing we can do is to keep asking, despite the invasive doubt and the memories of occasions when "the magic did not work," trusting that God is there in the situation itself and in our needy, fearful hearts.

A remarkable, parable-like story from the Old Testament reminds us what we are to do. The kingdom of Judah has been overrun (at the turn of the eighth century BCE) by the brutal Assyrian forces. Assyrian officials send a threatening message to Judah's king, Hezekiah. This is what happens next: "Hezekiah received the letter from the hand of the messengers and read it; then Hezekiah went up to the house of the Lord and spread it before the Lord. And Hezekiah prayed before the Lord, ..."[14] What to do with distress of mind and faintness of heart? "Spread it before the Lord"—or, as the old hymn says: "Take it to the Lord in prayer."

We must stay honest—this also is important—as to possibilities and impossibilities, doubts and fears, "no's" experienced as well as "yeses," concerning things prayed for.

We could open our minds to the idea of a relational God set forth earlier and reviewed here, in order that that we might better deal with perplexities deriving from the clash between certain traditional formulations and modern worldviews.

We could seek to open our imaginations, as well, to the model of prayer outlined here, and to its underlying idea that when we pray *to* God we are actually praying *in* God. In making the requests wrung from us by pressing concerns, we enter into an asking in which God the Spirit, as made known to us in Jesus Christ the "Son," participates—with "sighs too deep for words"—along with us. Prayer finds its essence, declares theologian Karl Rahner, when the word we speak to God is worked and spoken by [God] in us.[15]

And we could contemplate—once again—the simple but capacious truth that not only the impulse for our praying but also the ultimate *answer* are to be found in God's own presence and working in our lives. "The life of prayer is founded on prayer of petition," says Thomas Merton, a great modern spiritual master; but the ultimate outcome wished for would be that we might "be the place [God] has chosen for his presence, his manifestation in the world."[16]

The more we can learn to give ourselves to such a life of prayer, the more we will find prayer "changing things" and come to experience, even in the "yes *and* no" of our sinful, chancy, joyous-and-suffering lives, the "I *don't* mean maybe!" of a maturing faith.

ENDNOTES

[1] Articles such as the following—*Time* (June 24, 1996: "Faith and Healing," 59-64), *New Republic* (July 19 and 26, 1999: "Faith Healers: Is Religion Good for Your Health?"

20-23), and *Atlantic Monthly* (April, 2001: "Thy Will Be Done: Blind Studies and Answered Prayers," 18-20)—have drawn attention to medical research studies showing statistically significant relationships between (in some studies) worship service attendance and (in other studies) the practice of prayer and improved health: longer life spans, lower blood pressure, fewer bouts with depression, reduced risk of dying from coronary-artery disease, etc.

[2] 1 Samuel 12:23; James 5:16.

[3] Romans 12:12; 1 Thessalonians 5:17.

[4] Luke 18:1-8.

[5] Brother David Steindl-Rast, *Gratefulness, the Heart of Prayer: An Approach to Life in Fullness* (New York: Paulist Press, 1984), 100.

[6] Martin L. Smith SSJE, *The Word Is Very Near You: A Guide to Praying with Scripture* (Cambridge, Mass.: Cowley Publications: 1989), 14, 18ff.

[7] 2 Corinthians 5:19.

[8] Timothy Rees, "God is Love, let heaven adore him," in *The Hymnal 1982, according to the use of The Episcopal Church* (New York: Church Hymnal Corporation, 1982), hymn number 379.

[9] Romans 8:22-23, 26-27.

[10] Ephesians 3:20

[11] Remark made by Walter Wink, at a College of Preachers conference, Washington, DC, March 1996.

[12] Marjorie Hewitt Suchocki, *God—Christ—Church: A Practical Guide to Process Theology*, rev. ed. (New York: Crossroad, 1989), 224.

[13] Matthew 26:39.

[14] 2 Kings 19:14-15.

[15] Karl Rahner, *The Practice of Faith: A Handbook of Contemporary Spirituality* (New York: Crossroad, 1983), 86.

[16] Quoted in John J. Higgins, S.J., *Thomas Merton on Prayer* (Garden City, N.Y.: Doubleday, 1973), 83, 70.

CHAPTER SIX

Is Salvation "Accepting Jesus Christ as My Personal Savior"? And Other Questions about God as Liberator and Reconciler

The God who is self-revealing Presence, who continually creates and preserves all that is, who companions us in covenant faithfulness—why must this God also be spoken of as our "savior"? Why is it that one or another form of the word "salvation" meets us at every turn in our reading of Holy Scripture?

And how is it that salvation could be a matter of "accepting Jesus Christ as my personal savior"? The formula should be familiar, at least among those with a certain kind of Protestant background. Other emphases also, of course, demand consideration—especially the importance in several traditions of the church and its sacraments. But, for great numbers of people, any question about being "saved" brings to mind something like the invitation at the end of the message from the evangelist on television, which is always to "accept Christ," as "savior," and to make this an individual decision.

There is warrant for this—in experience and in Holy Scripture. What answer is given to the terrified jailer (in the story told in Acts) when he cries out, to the missionaries Paul and Silas, "What must I do to be saved?" "Believe on the Lord Jesus"—that is how they answer him—"believe, . . . and you will be saved, you and your household."[1]

And what does it mean that I myself, eleven years old at the time, knelt by a bunkbed in a "Bible Camp" in British Columbia and "let Jesus come into my heart as savior and Lord"? It doesn't mean anything that I would now repudiate; it was an authentic, life-changing decision.

But it also doesn't signify anything like the far-more-than-personal reality I have since come to believe is encompassed by the term "salvation." Which means that, along with the "yes" to be offered here, a careful "no" has also to be uttered—but in such a way that this can be followed, clearly and honestly, with an "and I *don't* mean maybe!"

Questions to be surveyed in this chapter include the following:

- Do we *need* "saving"? If we do, what are we to be saved *from*?
- Given the traditional Christian answer to that question—sin—what is meant by "sin"?
- (A parenthesis) Are we all "born in sin"? Do we participate in "original sin"?
- Why must it be *God* who saves us? And why Jesus Christ? (A topic to be further developed in the chapter following).
- What does it mean to speak of salvation as liberation? as reconciliation?
- Is salvation, then, "personal"?
- How can we combine "yes-*and*-no" answers to these issues of belief with a thoroughgoing "yes-and-I-*don't*-mean-maybe!" to the offer of salvation itself?

Do we need "saving"?

We need saving only if things have gone wrong. And then only if the solution seems not to lie entirely in our own hands. Is "the time . . . out of joint" for us, as Hamlet found it to be in the world imagined for him by William Shakespeare? If it be so, is it we alone in the universe who are—as it seemed Hamlet was—"born to set it right"?

Mixed Messages about the State of the World

Is our time "out of joint"? Current state-of-the-world reports offer mixed (no-and-yes) messages. We've never had it so good—that's one sound bite. These are prosperous times, in certain nations and for certain people within their borders. Relatively stable times, as well—again, for certain countries and their populations—despite the memory of September 11, 2001, the outbreak of problematic (and polarizing) wars, and the continuing threat of international terrorism.

Times of progress, many would want to add. In preventing and healing disease. In opening new avenues of communication, at least for those in a position to traverse the "information superhighway." In providing an abundance of products and services to enhance our lives, as well as an increased number of ways to "have fun." Even, perhaps, in meeting certain social and political needs of the human spirit.

And yet. And yet . . . . Listening more closely to these reports of prosperity, peace, and progress, do we not discern an undertone of indefinable sadness, a mystified sense of things gone awry?

One note is that of personal dissatisfaction, unfulfillment, deriving apparently from a persistent intimation of emptiness among many of those who supposedly "have it made." Numerous well-off men and women of our time seem to have become aware of that unanticipated poverty of soul. In an issue of the *New York Times Magazine* summarizing some of the findings of "The Way We Live Now" poll, one of the therapists participating in a colloquy moderated by Ariel Kaminer comments on the disappointment felt by a number of his ambitious, wealthy clients."They come into treatment," he says, "because of the emptiness that they feel."[2]

Every technological advance, furthermore—in communication, medicine, entertainment—turns out to have its downside. It seems we can do anything we set our minds to for betterment except alter, in those same minds, what turns to our detriment. Even the "worldwide web" is vulnerable to "viruses" that disrupt, and "chat rooms" that corrupt, this wonderful new interchange. And how are we to search out items of authentic value in a rapidly mounting heap of sheer triviality? "Where," as T. S. Eliot asked decades ago, "is the wisdom we have lost in knowledge? Where is the knowledge we have lost in information?"[3]

This abundance economy fosters such "trivial pursuits." Pursuits, as well, which are not so much trivial as downright harmful: addictions, to drugs or alcohol or gambling or overeating, that can seriously damage the one so enfettered and others in that person's network of relationship.

Miraculous new gadgets and games! And yet—marriages keep breaking up, even in households where the inhabitants lack nothing. At the other end of the income scale, the burden of single parenting grows ever harder to bear. Great numbers of children continue to be scarred by neglect or abuse.

On the larger stage, hate crimes are still with us. Terrorist attacks on a scale never before envisioned can virtually paralyze a powerful nation. Far too many of those representing us in government are being bought by corporate lobbyists ready to dole out vast sums of money. And the CEOs of those corporations, for their part, turn out to be so given over to profit that they will actually jeopardize the souls—sometimes the very lives—of those purchasing (not to mention those producing) their merchandise.

As for the environmental cost of our abundance—it is as if we are just now beginning to tune in on newscasts from the future concerning still-barely-imaginable catastrophes affecting the air we breathe, the water we drink, and even the climatic conditions on which every aspect of the ecological system ultimately depends.

Anyone with an ear for these fierce dissonances may well be haunted by anxiety, dogged by guilt. And falling back into apathy or cynically "opting out," will simply drive the anxiety and guilt underground, rendering the desperation more quiet, the soul-sickness more "low grade," but also more chronic and pervasive.

Divergent Views on Setting Things Right

Apathy will never quite win out. Ideas will always be floated, plans always put in place, for setting things right. What those ideas and plans consist of will depend on how the "wrongness" is understood. Some, offering a more radical analysis, will blame the "system" and advocate its overturn. Others want to insist we can just "fix" any problems that become apparent.

In our technology-dominated "can-do" culture, after all, the preferred strategy, across the board, is case-by-case problem-solving. Study the problem, find the resources needed, and "fix" the malfunctioning element—whether the economy, or a family unit, or a particular institution, or even a mind with a worldview that needs remodeling or a soul that finds itself disturbed, or simply unhappy.

A Christian "Yes-and-No" Perspective on What Goes Wrong and How It Can be Set Right

A Christian social critic could say "yes" to both of these responses—changing the system and fixing particular defects—while also identifying a disabling omission. What has been left out is the reality of *sin*, a power that can cause us to become blind to divine presence, destructive of God's creation, and, in various ways, cut off from the "love that moves the sun and the other stars."[4] As the Apostle Paul insists, "All have sinned and *fall short of the glory of God*."[5]

A second-century Christian thinker, Irenaeus, carries the thought further. "The glory of God," he tells us, "is a human being fully alive."[6] Sin, then, would encompass anything causing us to be off the mark of what it means fully to be God's creatures. To say that ours is a sinful state is to say both that things in us and our world are not as they should be and that some responsibility for this ultimately falls on us.

Whatever it is that can save us must take on every system with which our lives are bound up, but it must also go deeper. It must make room for all the techniques and programs human ingenuity can contrive, but it must touch us more radically, as well. Otherwise we remain creatures who, as T. S. Eliot puts it,

> constantly try to escape
> From the darkness outside and within
> By dreaming of systems so perfect that no one will need
> to be good.[7]

(A Parenthesis): Are we "born in sin," enmeshed in "Original Sin"?

It is always easy to underestimate the power and the prevalence of sinfulness. It was in order to insist on the all-pervading nature of this tendency to go wrong and the universal need of divine redemption that the doctrine of "Original Sin" was thought out.

According to this teaching—formulated most cogently by Augustine, a North African bishop ofthe early fifth century—we are sinful from birth. As descendants of Adam—the Apostle Paul tells us—we participate in Adam's "original" act of disobedience.[8] In Augustine's reading, this would mean that the propensity to sinfulness, along with the guilt sin brings with it, is passed along at conception.

The Need to Say "No" to the Doctrine of Original Sin

This teaching, which gravely misrepresents both the saving goodness of God and our human freedom of choice, rests on several mistaken interpretations of biblical passages. The saying in Psalm 51, for instance (especially as translated in the centuries-old King James Version of the Bible): "In sin did my mother conceive me."[9]

Or the teachings of Paul already mentioned. And, most of all, the story of the "Fall," in Genesis chapter 3, read as if there really was an Adam and an Eve, they really did listen to the blandishments of a tempter, and a "curse" was visited on them which falls on us their "descendants" as well; read literally, in other words, not as a *story* conveying truth but a factual, historical account.

In view of the misreadings of Scripture and the undervaluing of human freedom—not to mention the pre-scientific genetics—bound up with this doctrine, we have every right to insist that every newborn enters the world not borne down by "original sin" but, as theologian Matthew Fox puts it, gifted with "original blessing."[10]

But "Yes," As Well, to the Notion of Original Sin

A "yes" can also be said. This is not to affirm the doctrine as promulgated for centuries by certain representatives of the church, but to point toward indispensable truths of which that teaching nevertheless reminds us.

The doctrine directs us toward an irresolvable mystery, an obvious fact, and a saving truth. The mystery? That we act, in ourselves and toward others, as if we are free to choose aright, and therefore responsible, to some degree, for our actions. That we find ourselves, at the same time, not free not to choose what is wrong for us and for others. "I delight in the law of God in my inmost self," Paul writes, "but I see in my members another law . . . , making me captive to the law of sin that dwells in my members."[11]

The obvious fact? That, whether or not we are born *in* sin we are born *into* sin: into a system of systems—social, political, economic, intellectual systems—riddled with wrong habits and wrong dispositions: a web of potentiality for both evil and good spun over millennia of human history and pre-history. So that sin is "original" at least in this regard, that before *our* origin sin has had *its* origin in the world we now find to be ours. Given, then, the accumulated force of the many "no's" already spoken within all the systems into which we are born—and given the mystery of freedom and unfreedom within us—each of us sooner or later, without fail, even though not by necessity, follows suit, thus becoming part of the "all" in Paul's sweeping pronouncement: "All have sinned, and come short of the glory of God."

The saving truth is that of divine grace. For St. Paul's notion of our identification with Adam as primal transgressor takes second place to the affirmation that we find salvation "in Christ." This "one man's act of righteousness leads to justification and life for all."[12]

What does it mean to say we are being "saved" from "sin"?

Each of our responses to divine Love either draws the world toward fulfillment of the divine vision or brings about a diminishing or distorting of possibilities. Which means that the feelings accompanying our response in any new moment may be lighted up with enthusiasm or shaded with chagrin, even bitter, tragic sadness.

These feelings are not just ours, either. We are also tuning in, at some frequency, to God's "feelings" of us. This divine evaluation registers us both in our "glory" and "with all [our] imperfections on [our] head." *And* as we could have been at that moment, had we responded more fully and freely to some divinely-granted opening for works of love and justice.

We experience this contrast between the is and the could-have-been as some gradation of "judgment." Something in us says—what Christian worshipers regularly say in their shared Confession—"We have not loved you with our whole heart; we have not loved our neighbors as ourselves."

> A character in a novel by Albert Camus describes an ingenious instrument of torture from the Middle Ages called the little-ease. The little-ease was a dungeon cell not high enough to stand up in nor wide enough to sit down in. A captive in this cell could never be at rest; specific pain would give way to a general aching and then to all-absorbing agony. "Through the unchanging restriction of the little-ease," says this narrative voice, "the condemned man learned that he was guilty." But he also learned, the speaker goes on, "that innocence consists in stretching joyously."[13]

The word of salvation is that divine love is unending, divine creativity unquenchable, "stretching joyously" always possible. The God who knows us as we are over against what we could have been senses us also, in any moment, as what we could yet be. When a creative vision of possibility is thwarted by our sinful response, other gracious invitations from God can open new, "saving" possibilities.

Salvation as the Restoration of our Capacity to Know God in All Things

The divine reality, it was affirmed in Chapter One, becomes known to us as self-revealing presence, inviting us to know God in all things and know all things in God.

We are in sin, therefore, when we exist as if there were no God to be known, screening out, or misperceiving, the "otherness," the "beyond" in things. The Apostle Paul speaks of those who, "though they knew God, . . . did not honor him as God or give thanks to him, but . . . became futile in their thinking, and their senseless minds were darkened."[14]

Whenever we suppress intimations of divine presence, we are in danger of "tuning out" much of the fierce energy and tender beauty of nature, or the "glorious exchanges" of life in community, or the subtle truth conveyed by way of music and poetry, or the insights granted the soul in its intervals of meditation and thought.

Much in our modern, "secular" way of life helps bring this about—what has come to be spoken of as "consumerism," for example, or a quasi-addiction to TV viewing or internet-surfing. "The world is too much with us," wrote William Wordsworth two centuries ago;

> late and soon,
> Getting and spending, we lay waste our powers;

> Little we see in Nature that is ours;
> We have given our hearts away, ...

And then? Some simply settle for this "flatness" in existence, this inclination always to "use" things for ourselves rather than also to pause and contemplate them as they are in their God-given intricate beauty. Others of us attempt to enliven things with "thrills"—our own, or those of celebrities whose triumphs and downfalls we avidly follow. Or to cover the hazardous silences by way of small talk and gossip.

And God moves to save us. How? By way of the "signs" identified in Chapter One. We find ourselves "spoken to" from something in nature, or in relationships of love and friendship, or by way of the visionary creations of musicians or poets or thinkers, or through subtle intimations from the seemingly far-off interior of our being. For that moment, at least, some glory that has departed comes back into view, some broken line of connection hums with power once again.

All of which brings up, also, the question of the Bible. The potentially "saving" work of God through nature, and other persons, and historical-cultural memory as reflected on in individual consciousness is illuminated for us by the biblical stories and images and insights that have informed so much of our sense of things.

But it must also be declared—once again—that our Bible-reading itself is in need of salvation. God's saving grace must touch the trafficking between the text of the Bible and us its interpreters. Otherwise, the God we profess to know through what "the Bible says" can become not a saving reality but—in the sinfully biased image of implacable judge, or ruthless warrior, or dominating father-figure (or, more recently, that helpful "nice guy" "upstairs")—a fiercely, or blandly, destructive idol.

Salvation as the Recovery of our "Glory" as Creatures of God

Salvation is not just about knowledge and awareness. And no vague, tenuous notion of "God" can represent the true and sufficient object of such a search. For the God present to the world is also actively in relationship with the world, as its creator and preserver, and in a particular kind of relationship with the human creation. Genesis chapter 2 informs us, by way of a notable image, that we are brought into being by God's "breath," or (the same word in Hebrew) "spirit," and upheld therein until, as the Psalmist puts it, simply, naively, God "takes away [our] breath," so that we "die and return to [our] dust."[15]

Within the intermeshing freedoms of the created order, we are offered a way of being-in-the-world that is imbued with trust, expectancy, appreciativeness, festivity and play, desire for community, productiveness, and the acceptance of creaturely limits, including that final limit: our mortality.

In actuality, however, vast numbers have been traumatized into profound anxiety. Those caught up in heartless, exploitative systems—how can they wait expectantly for anything better than what they have known: scrabbling for a bare subsistence by means of debilitating labor or pitiful hand-outs? Those dispossessed and exiled by hate-driven conflict—how can they come to know the comforting predictabilities that characterize life in community, or find personal soul-space for the shaping of creative work to gladden hearts?

For these "wretched of the earth," then, salvation has to involve not only transformation of individual character and disposition but also some degree of *liberation* from that in the system which would leave elemental human needs unmet and essential human powers undeveloped.[16]

The same system, however, that consigns men, women, and children in some parts of the world and some echelons of society to a soul-crippling misery can, in other regions or at other class levels, enslave many in soul-shrinking affluence. As Andrew Delbanco writes, in the *New York Times Magazine* feature already referred to, "Abundance and freedom can bewilder as well as liberate, and many Americans . . . are reverting to William James's view that 'happiness in the absolute and everlasting is what we find nowhere but in religion.'"[17]

How can the vision of a restored capability for freedom and joy as creatures of God be realized? What does God provide for us and ask of us? Clues can be found in some of the most ancient-seeming stories in the Bible's "book of beginnings" (Genesis): those "Sunday School" stories of which the first, and most famous concerns Adam and Eve.

There is a pattern to this primal story. That pattern, writes biblical scholar Walter Brueggemann, includes a calling, a permission, and a prohibition. As God's human creation, we are *called* to walk with God following the ways of God, caring for one another and for all creatures.

This calling is fulfilled in *freedom*: We are to "do it our way," creatively or destructively. At the same time, we are made aware of *limits*—not the arbitrary "Don't touch, or I'll slap your hand!" of this very sophisticated and yet childlike story, but the always essential reality of limits on behavior, whether through individual conscience or the rules and laws and constitution of a community.[18]

Here in Genesis, and elsewhere in Holy Scripture as well, we are made aware, at the same time, of saving possibilities offered where sinful men and women have exercised their freedom to violate some "prohibition," thereby falling short of the "glory" of their "calling." Again and again we are offered the saving wisdom that can enable a return to the creaturely ways by which we fulfill God's glory and our own.

As in this realm of inspired folklore, so it is in our all-too-real history. To those suffering at the hands of persons and systems violating the fundamental "rules" for human life together come opportunities, from time to time, for overthrowing the oppressors, or reforming the system, or—at the least—creating within the dehumanizing larger society enclaves of peace and creativity. With regard to certain happenings within the lifetime of many of us—the end of Communist domination in Eastern Europe, the victory over South Africa's deadly Apartheid policies, and widespread dramatic changes in the status of women—believers can only exclaim, with the psalmist, "This is the Lord's doing; it is marvelous in our eyes."[19]

Something like these saving transformations happens in individual lives as well. Alcoholics or other addicts stumble into a "tough-love" Twelve-Step program and, despite inevitable slips and falls, break free after decades of enslavement. Persons encased with "character armor" or weighed down with chronic depression are guided to a therapist in whose care they find a measure of healing. Battered wives receive courage to leave abusive men; batterers finally consent to the self-scrutiny and behavioral change they so profoundly need.

What such happenings mean is this: To be one of God's human creatures is to know that things have gone wrong, that we are both victims of the sins of others and, in some way, sinners ourselves, "falling short" of the "glory" meant to be ours. It is to sense, also, that the saving possibilities of "amazing grace" are always open to us and always—even now, even here—at work.

Salvation as Reconciliation with God as Covenant Partner

For those at all aware of the invitation to be "covenant partners" with God (the theme of Chapter Four), sin consists also in our refusing some aspect of this relationship. The self-revealing reality that creates and provides for all things desires, as well, our companionship: "I will be your God, and you shall be my people." Such a God, under the limited but still valid images of "king," "father" (and "mother"), "judge," and "friend," provides the gifts of divine authority, wisdom, guidance, friendship.

The sin of rejecting such an invitation to covenant companionship can afflict the soul with a sense of estrangement from the sources of all that is best in life. "Your iniquities," the prophet Isaiah tells his hearers, "have become barriers between you and your God."[20] And if, in the words of Abraham Heschel with which Chapter Four began,

"God means no one is ever alone," our persistent loneliness in the world may be another sign of that state of sinfulness.

The obligations attendant upon the covenant walk with God include, as already mentioned, commandments taken to be gracious aids to the full realization of our humanity. Some seek to prevent us from harming ourselves. Others govern behavior toward our "neighbors": don't do violence against them, or steal from them, or cheat them, or speak words to their detriment.[21] All of them reflect what is understood to be God's desire that we should be "human beings fully alive." And we transgress these rules by way of specific, identifiable "sins."

In such a context, sin is revealed to be, most profoundly, about us and God. "Against you alone have I sinned," one of the psalmists writes, in that great prayer of penitence which is Psalm 51, "and done what is evil in your sight."[22]

Salvation here centers on making right what has gone wrong in human life through specific transgressions. Wrongdoing is not just going against "the way things are supposed to be," it is an offence against a just and loving God. And salvation requires more than just "getting things right this time"; it calls for "getting right with God."

Such a salvation comes through the loving power of a God who is reconciler as well as liberator. It requires much more of us than "fixing things" in our systems or our selves. It requires that, on the way to healing, we make our way through what the tradition calls "judgment." For it is only when that divine love and judgment sink deep into the very core of our created being that sadness can turn into joy, enslavement into freedom, emptiness into abundant life, guilty estrangement into reconcilement and restoration.

> A number of years ago, I was called upon to give spiritual counsel to a man dying of ALS. A longtime "home Baptist," this man was tormented by guilt over past wrongdoing and needed assurance of forgiveness. Communication was limited to statements and questions from me and eye-movement responses on his part.
>
> This was salvation at its most basic. With agonizing slowness, over a period of weeks, I put questions to him about past actions for which he felt remorse, secured his acknowledgment of penitence, and passed on to him my vision of God as (in the words of Psalm 103) "merciful and gracious, . . . and abounding in steadfast love."[23]

> When the end drew near, I found an appropriate way to "give absolution," in the assurance of God's saving love as embodied in Jesus, and thus assure him of reconciliation with a God who both judges and forgives "all [our] iniquity."

(A Parenthesis): Is salvation, then, to be understood as "personal" salvation?

Failing fully to be "covenant partners" with God is the form of sinfulness that can be identified most clearly as "personal." Does it follow that salvation from such sin has also to be a "personal" salvation?

A Cautionary "No" to Salvation as "Personal"

In our time many have come to view salvation as a matter almost entirely of individual feelings and attitudes and personal decision. Privatized religion, however, too easily neglects the sinfulness present in systems rather than merely individuals—in governments, corporations, institutions (including, undeniably, the church itself!). What stands in need of divine salvation includes corporate entities as well as individual selves.

Which means that God's saving intention can be discerned in efforts to bring elements of society, government, and the economy under the rule of God's justice. Where authentically humane "liberation" movements are underway, then—in Africa, the United States, Latin America, anywhere—Christian believers can rejoice in such endeavors. And rejoice regardless of whether the leaders of these movements have ever "signed on" as "believers."

Privatized religion also too easily undervalues the role of the "institutional" *church*—and its beliefs—in all the forms salvation can take. But for Christians, as affirmed everywhere in the New Testament and in tradition through the centuries, participation in the life of the church is very much a part of the economy of salvation.

But "Yes," as Well, to "Personal" Salvation

We don't have to think very long about systems to realize the obvious: that it is individual *persons* who are members of families and communities and who staff banks and schools and transnational corporations, and houses of Congress. It's not hard to see, as well, that change in such bodies cannot keep happening without individual commitment to such reforms.

In any case, God's saving intention is not limited to peoples and nations and institutions. God deals with the "small stuff" of human selves just as much as with the "big jobs" emerging in human systems. If God is in relation to us, those creatures capable of becoming persons, the salvation offered us in God will have to be, in some respects, a "personal" salvation, depending upon individual decisions in response to divine grace.

Such authentic transformation requires radical change at the core of one's being. This is why the tradition—listening to voices like that of the prophet Jeremiah and Jesus and the Apostle Paul—is so clear about the need for a "new heart," or a "new birth," or (in Paul's formulation): a "new creation" in Christ.[24]

Salvation does mean "accepting . . . [a] personal savior." It does entail being "born again." *How* this happens is another matter. A single life-changing "evangelical"-style conversion experience (like mine at the bible camp so many years ago) is one way. A happening like that which Dag Hammarskjøld described in his journal—"At some moment I did answer *Yes* to Someone—or Something—and from that hour I was certain that existence is meaningful and that, therefore, my life, in self-surrender, had a goal."[25]—is another possibility. For the steady "catholic"-type church-attender—baptized as a child, receiving the Sacrament and hearing the Word read and preached every Sunday—there may be no one saving decision, perhaps, but a series of small responses to quiet promptings from the Spirit during gatherings for worship or times of private prayer.

But conversion, in some sense, there must be. And repentance, as part of it. There has to be, from time to time—as suggested in the very origins of that term *conversion*—a "turning," a change of path. To be in process of personal salvation is to be ready to turn away from ("repent of": change one's mind about) something discerned (under "judgment") as counter to the divine intention, and turn toward ("convert to") a life path illumined with the divine vision of a just and neighborly world.

What does it mean to speak of Jesus as "savior"?

Salvation is something to be "accepted," "personally." But Jesus? Why should it be Jesus that is accepted? Because special consideration is given to this topic in the chapter following, only a sketch of an answer will be included here, in order that the picture of salvation provided in the present chapter will not be left seriously incomplete.

"Yes and *No" to the Declaration that "Jesus Saves"*

"Jesus saves"? No; it is God, and only God, who saves. That's what a devout Jew would have to say in reponse to such a statement of faith. A Muslim likewise. And Christians would agree: God is our only savior. But Christians would identify this divine savior as "the God and Father of our Lord Jesus Christ."[26]

And this is where a "yes" can be brought forward—at this point only in outline—in answer to the question about Jesus and God's saving work in the world. Jesus is, to begin with, an authentic image of our humanity "in its glory." All the characteristics previously identified as the birthright of all God's human creatures and marked as under threat of sinful distortion can be seen fulfilled, "without sin," in the Jesus set before us in the New Testament.

Jesus is also, for us, the agent and embodiment of God's saving work. It is in Jesus as the Christ that God is "reconciling the world," releasing us from sin's enslavement, shaping us in the "image of God" according to which we are created and which is seen in fullness in "the man Christ Jesus."[27]

The witness of the gospels to the career of Jesus says something also, however—and overwhelmingly—about human sinfulness, about stubborn resistance to the divine promise. So many rejected the teachings outright. So many, in fear, left the way they had begun to traverse. So many of those closest to Jesus misunderstood—and so many have since misrepresented—the import of what he taught. Some even followed out the wicked impulse to silence the disturbing voice, by arranging the arrest, the trial and humiliation, the death on a cross.

But Jesus has become, also—as the "risen one"—the continuing presence, for faith, of the "Word made flesh." The God who saves is the God who was present in Jesus of Nazareth and continues to be present in the spirit of the crucified-and-risen Christ. And we are saved through identifying ourselves with the vision of realized humanity in Jesus and with the sinful humanity of his crucifiers, while receiving for ourselves the reconciling, liberating, renewing presence of God in Jesus. This is how we "accept Jesus Christ as personal savior."

"Yes" to God's *offer* of salvation; "yes *and* no" to certain *teachings about* salvation?

To say "yes" to God's offer of salvation is to affirm certain beliefs concerning the relationship between God and humankind put forward earlier in this book as well as within this chapter.

Belief Questions Demanding a "Yes"

God's saving grace, it needs first to be said, is being made available, to persons and to systems disordered by sinfulness, always and everywhere. Salvation is not just something that happens in church; it happens in the midst of a tribal confrontation in Africa, or in an inner-city project anywhere on the globe, or in a debate within some governmental body concerning its most neglected constituents; it happens for a drunk finally "hitting bottom" and going for help, or a household that has been for years embittered by resentful quarreling, as well as for a young woman following out her heart's impulse to return to the church of her childhood.

It is also true that we are saying a certain "yes" to salvation in the very act of existing with some degree of authenticity within a society that is, in significant ways, sick and disheartened. A film-maker is saying "yes" in producing work that offers glimpses of redemption. A worker is saying "yes" in taking up the cause, within the union local, of improving pay and conditions among demoralized minimum-wage fellow-workers. A distracted salesclerk or mother-of-toddlers is saying "yes" by setting aside a patch of time each day for opening her inner world, in silence, to the Spirit of God.

Salvation happens in relationship: this is the third point to be made. It happens in order to set relationships right—relationship with God, fellow human beings, and the non-human creation. Archbishop Tutu was furthering salvation-as-reconcilement when he made it possible for the enforcers of South Africa's racist policy of Apartheid to confess their brutalities before the Truth and Reconciliation Commission. Saving moments occur in families, again and again, where estranged members find the courage to ask and receive forgiveness.

And what happens in salvation? "Accepting Jesus as personal savior," we offer ourselves to a process whereby we are being liberated from what enslaves us and reconciled with that from which we are estranged. This comes about through our receiving from God a new quality of life enabling us to love others and ourselves and to enact that love by working as co-creators and co-providers with God.

Downtrodden people can find themselves on a path to liberation—overcoming their inner sense of themselves as inferior and working to reform the outer structures of an oppressive society. Individual transformation is also possible, for victims of addiction, as well as for persons crippled by habitual resentment or prejudice. Or for aging men and women, sensing that now (in the words of poet William Carlos Williams) "the descent beckons, as the ascent beckoned,"[28] but finding the grace of acceptance for themselves and a deepened joy in grasping the hands of others on the same descent but unready and filled with fear.

Belief Questions Asking a "Yes **and** *No"*

Certain questions requiring such a "yes-*and*-no" response have already been addressed: "Is salvation 'personal'?" was one of these; "Is salvation a matter of a once-for-all conversion experience?" another. One vital question—"Is Jesus *the* way to salvation?"—is to be taken up later. But several concerns remain to be dealt with.

Is salvation the same thing as "*rescue*"?—that's one such question. Rescue is undeniably what many people are asking for when they call out to God for salvation. Even Jesus is remembered as having cried out to be delivered from the time of trial: "Abba, Father, for you all things are possible; remove this cup from me."[29]

Salvation *can* mean rescue: divine love seeks always the well-being of all creatures. But the divine freedom acts continually in relation to other freedoms; so that often a disablement has become so entrenched or a disease so advanced, or relations between peoples so strained, that no way can be found but one involving suffering and loss.

What if the answer to the question about "rescue" is "yes *and* no"? This is the divine response Paul discerned to his entreaties concerning the mysterious "thorn in his flesh" mentioned in the second letter to the Corinthians: "But [the Lord] said to me, 'My grace is sufficient for you, for power is made perfect in weakness.'"[30] It is the experience of Jesus, as well, who was *not* spared the humiliation and agony he dreaded but after his death nevertheless "rose again"; that is, entered new life in God and was experienced as lovingly, lifegivingly present among those gathered for worship and at work in the world in his name. For salvation is not merely something that comes *from* God; it is God's own presence. God does not always save us *from* suffering—as someone has wisely said—but God can always save us *in* our suffering.

A "yes *and* no" has also to be said to the question: Do we not save *ourselves*? A "no" answer would seem unavoidable; salvation is God's doing for us something we cannot do for ourselves. And yet—as already suggested—God's saving work is performed through human agency. So a "yes" answer to this question about salvation speaks of what constitutes a faithful response to God's saving invitation.

For we *are* free to open ourselves to signs of divine presence. We can enter into that "larger story," identifying our own stories with its saving elements. "Working out" such openings—with appropriate degrees of "fear and trembling" (to recall, once again, Paul's words)—we give God plenty to "work with" in prompting decisions on our part by which we welcome God's saving grace.[31]

A final question comes with a certain edge to it: Isn't salvation, after all, mainly about making us "good people"? And if it is, how can it be said that we are being saved when sinful behavior is still so prevalent, even in the lives of those who call themselves Christians?

"No" has to be the answer, initially, to such a question. No, we do not fully triumph over the inclination to sin nor, necessarily, over certain sinful attitudes or habits. To be saved *from* sin is to be saved, also, *in* sin. Self-centered persons who have become believers may abuse their created freedom by indulging residues of selfishness. Addicts seeking God's saving help may find themselves unable fully to overcome the disabling habit. The success of a great liberation movement may be followed by a chapter in history that is thoroughly disheartening.

But the question can also be responded to with a valid "yes." Why? Because salvation is not, first of all, about "making people good." It is about bringing people into a fundamentally right relationship with God and, potentially, with one another. The mark of living by faith is not so much that we regularly "get things right" as that we are ready to open ourselves to getting it right: by availing ourselves continually of God's forgiveness and reempowerment.

It is also true, of course, that if we stay in touch to any degree with this power of divine love we *will* become "better persons." Only, let's not be the ones seeking to make that judgment! Perhaps the Danish philosopher Søren Kierkegaard can be our model here: Though now perceived as one of the jewels in the crown of Christian character, he consistently refused to speak of himself as "a Christian," declaring himself, rather, one "seeking to become a Christian."[32]

And a Final, Difficult "Yes and I Don't *Mean Maybe!"*

What does it mean, in the face of such perplexities, to say, nevertheless, concerning acceptance of the offer of salvation, "Yes and I *don't* mean maybe"?

It means choosing to live for God, wholeheartedly, even while living, as honestly as possible, with these tensions. In the face of conflicting views, we are to take the risk, nonetheless, of "standing" (as the old gospel hymn has it) "on the promises of God."

It means, therefore, staying in touch with those "promises" of salvation, as found preeminently in Holy Scripture. Some of these come in the form of salvation stories about the people Israel—stories of liberation from enslavement, of wandering and arrival, of joyous return after long exile. Some appear by way of images: the image of healing for those despairing of life; of reconcilement, between ruler and subject, between brothers, and (according to the parable in Luke chapter 15) between wronged parent and "prodigal" son; of new life flowing into bones bleaching in the wilderness (in the prophetic vision of Ezekiel chapter 37), and—the core teaching of the New Testament witness—of a crucified-and-risen Christ, made present to the world with God's own power to liberate, reconcile, and endow with new life all who ask in faith.

There are, as well, the great sayings. Anyone "taking refuge" (as a Buddhist might say) in the Bible can unearth innumerable "promises"—like the affirmation of 1 Peter 1:3 (to give only one example) that "the God and Father of our Lord Jesus Christ . . . has given us a new birth into a living hope through the resurrection of Jesus Christ from the dead"—promises on which one's beleaguered heart can "stand" and in which one's burdened soul can rest.

As suggested in Chapter Four, anyone who would respond to God with a "yes and I *don't* mean maybe" must "take refuge" also in observance—which most often means involvement in a community of faith. A good part of what Jesus did, according to the gospels, was to form a cadre of learners by whom his message could be reflected on and spread abroad; and much of the rest of the New Testament concerns the emergence of a body of believing men and women called the "church" who (according to Acts chapter 2) "were together and had all things in common" and who "devoted themselves to the apostles' teaching and fellowship, to the breaking of bread and the prayers."[33]

Salvation does turn out to be, after all, a matter of "accepting Jesus Christ as 'personal savior.'" How complex the process designated in those simple words can be has been in good part the subject of the chapter now concluded. But complexities yet remain. Salvation in Jesus means immersing ourselves—with a "yes and I *don't* mean maybe!" despite all the "yes-*and*-no" perplexities—in the reality of Jesus' life and death and resurrection, as that reality is made accessible to us; and identifying our lives with that life and death and resurrection, insofar as such identification, or participation, is possible for us.

These engaging but daunting mysteries—accepting a Christ who "died for us"; dying and rising with Jesus Christ—are the subject of further reflections on God as liberator and reconciler in the chapter which follows.

ENDNOTES

[1] Acts 16:30-31.

[2] "What Do We Talk About When We are Paying Someone to Listen?"—a colloquy

among six therapists, moderated by Ariel Kaminer,—*New York Times Magazine* (May 7, 2000), 83.

[3] T. S. Eliot, "Choruses from *The Rock*," in *The Complete Poems and Plays 1909-1950* (New York: Harcourt, Brace, and Co., 1952), 96.

[4] The phrase with which each section ends, in Dante Alighieri's *Divine Comedy*, trans. Charles S. Singleton (Princeton, N.J.: Princeton University Press, 1973).

[5] Romans 3:23.

[6] Cited by numerous theologians; here, by way of Fritjov Capra and David Steindl-Rast, *Belonging to the Universe: Explorations on the Frontiers of Science and Spirituality* (HarperSanFrancisco, 1991), 147.

[7] Eliot, "Choruses," 106.

[8] Romans 5:12.

[9] Psalm 51:5.

[10] Matthew Fox, *The Coming of the Cosmic Christ: The Healing of Mother Earth and the Birth of a Global Renaissance* (San Francisco: Harper and Row, 1988), 82.

[11] Romans 7:21-23.

[12] Romans 5:18-19.

[13] Albert Camus, *The Fall*, trans. Justin O'Brien (New York: Vintage Books, 1956), 109-10.

[14] Romans 1:21.

[15] Genesis 2:7; Psalm 104:29.

[16] The meaning of sin and salvation with regard to such oppressive systems—whether having to do with class, or race, or gender—is the special purview of the "Liberation Theologies" emerging in recent decades in Latin America, Asia, and other regions. Representative Liberationist theologians would include: (Latin American theologians) Gustavo Gutierrez, Leonardo Boff, Jon Sobrino; (American Feminist theologians) Rosemary Radford Ruether and Elisabeth Schussler Fiorenza.

[17] Andrew Delbanco, "Are You Happy Yet?" *New York Times Magazine* (May 7, 2000), 48.

[18] Walter Brueggemann, *Genesis* (Atlanta: John Knox Press, l982), 46.

[19] Psalm 118:23.

[20] Isaiah 59:2.

[21] Exodus 20:13-17.

[22] Psalm 51:4.

[23] Psalm 103:8.

[24] 2 Corinthians 5:17.

[25] Dag Hammarskjøld, *Markings*, trans. Leif Sjøberg and W. H. Auden (New York: Ballantine Books, 1964), 180.

[26] 1 Peter 1:3.

[27] 2 Corinthians 5:17-18; 4:4-6.

[28] William Carlos Williams, "The Descent," *Pictures from Brueghel and Other Poems: Collected Poems 1950-1962* (New York: New Directions, 1962), 73.

[29] Mark 14:36.

[30] 2 Corinthians 12:7b-9.

[31] Philippians 2:12-13.

[32] Walter Lowrie—in his 2-volume work *Kierkegaard* (New York: Harper and Brothers, Harper Torchbook ed., 1962), 391—remarks that "becoming a Christian" was an "expression which Soren Kierkegaard persisted in using about himself."

It must also be brought to mind that many who claim the title "Christian"—especially when the term designates political or quasi-political groupings—manifest zero commitment to what salvation through Christ might mean in their life practice.
[33] Acts 2:42.

CHAPTER SEVEN

Did Jesus "Die for Our Sins"? More Questions about God as Liberator and Reconciler

Even the meaning ascribed to the name of the first-century teacher and wonder-worker from Nazareth in Galilee is meant to establish his identity as savior. In Matthew's story of the birth, an angel declares that this child of Mary is to be called "Jesus"; that is, "he will save." As one who "will save his people from their sins," Jesus is not only to convey a prophetic message *about* a new divine saving event; Jesus, in his own person, is to *be* that saving event.[1]

But what about the truth that only God can save? The continuation of the angelic message to Joseph touches on this question as well. A prophetic oracle concerning a special birth centuries earlier is brought into connection with this nativity, through the name assigned to that earlier child of promise: "Emmanuel," which means, "God is with us."[2] The implication is that the human being named Jesus in whom God's redemptive power is at work must also participate *in* that divine reality.

Accordingly, "accepting Jesus Christ as one's personal savior"—the topic of the previous chapter—requires a fundamental response to the meaning of the happenings spoken of as the "crucifixion" and the "resurrection," as well as the significance of Jesus' teachings and remarkable healings. The question, to use one of the traditional formulations, is this: Did Jesus die "for our sins"? Or, thinking of the relationship between the dying-and-rising Jesus and a God bringing salvation: Did Jesus "have to die" in order for us to be saved?

Questions to be taken up in this chapter include the following:

- Is Jesus *the* way to God's salvation?
- Is/was Jesus God?
- Did Jesus "have to" die?
- Did Jesus have to "rise from the dead"?
- Can we say "yes *and* no" to certain questions of belief about Jesus

as savior and yet say "I *don't* mean maybe" to the crucified-and-risen Jesus who offers to *be* our savior?

(A Preliminary Question): Is Jesus *the only* way to God's salvation?

Why Jesus? *Is* Jesus "the way, and the truth, and the life"? Must it be insisted that "no one comes to the Father except through [Jesus]?"[3] In strictly personal terms this question means: Do *I* have to "accept Jesus" in order to be "saved"? Can I not choose some other available path? More generally, the question—for believing Christians—is: Must certain *other* persons, adherents of other religions, also find their salvation only in Jesus?

Let this second question be taken up first, then, and let the first answer be "no." No, to the ancient dictum: "There is no salvation outside the church." No, to the purely exclusivist reading of the assertion attributed to the Apostle Peter: "There is salvation in no one else, for there is no other name under heaven given among mortals by which we must be saved."[4]

No, for reasons already given. It is of the very nature of God to be in creative, redemptive relation to everything that is. What is going on on the Godward side, furthermore, is always taking account of circumstances at any particular time or in any particular region and always addressing, and responding to, human freedom.

God's saving grace, therefore, can manifest itself in different forms in the Far East and on the Indian subcontinent than at the eastern end of the Mediterranean or in those regions later spoken of as Europe. The Apostle Peter says something like this in a sermon recollected in Acts: "God shows no partiality, but in every nation anyone who fears him and does what is right is acceptable to him."[5] Marjorie Suchocki makes the same point in theological terms: "Jesus reveals the boundless grace of God," she reminds us, "but to say that the grace is boundless is to say that we cannot set up the limits of that grace."[6]

The question "Is Jesus *the* way to God?" can be put to a simple practical test: Would we really have wanted the devout Hindu Mahatma Gandhi to become a convert to Christianity? Should the Dalai Lama forswear Tibetan Buddhism and become a Catholic monk? Does not the character-portrait of Muhammad that has come down to us compare in "the beauty of holiness" with that of many Christian saints?

Such a list of exemplars brings with it, however, a reminder that this "no" to the question about salvation in Jesus must not be a too-easy, spiritually lazy response. To say that salvation can be reached by a number of routes is not to say that "anything goes": "you can believe what you believe and I'll believe what I believe, and we'll all be OK." All who would come to God must be serious seekers, learning to open hearts and minds to the ultimate love-compassion-wisdom that alone frees us from the grip of the "wrongness" called sin and enables the realization of our created glory.

This is where a "yes" answer begins to emerge, as well. Is Jesus *the* way to God's salvation? In a sense, for those nurtured within a Christian—rather than some other—tradition the answer has to be "yes." The symbols and stories and concepts associated with Jesus as savior pervade certain societies and their cultures. Any persons at all serious about religion who have grown up in one of those regions will be drawn to conceive of a saving God in terms deriving from Christian teachings about Jesus.

Such persons will be well advised, then, to explore their religious homeland—with open minds and ready hearts—before charting a journey to (seemingly) more exotic territories. For they will discover that Paul was right to declare that none of us needs to be "ashamed of the gospel; it is the power of God for salvation to everyone who has faith."[7] They will also come to realize that our acceptance of Jesus Christ can encompass, as well, enrichment through many of the beliefs and practices of other religions.

As for those following other paths to salvation—without turning other beliefs and practices into disguised versions of Christianity, Christians can affirm, with theologian Schubert Ogden, "not that God acts to redeem only in the history of Jesus and in no other history, but that the only God who redeems any history . . . is the God whose redemptive action is decisively re-presented in the word that Jesus speaks and is."[8] And, following Archbishop Rowan Williams' counsel, they can "respond to the work of human salvage and restoration wherever it occurs by 'naming' it as Christ's work."[9]

Was Jesus God?

The "how" questions begin here. Only God can save. If, in the words of an old gospel song, "*Jesus* saves," then would not Jesus have to "be God"? To this question, asked that way, the answer has, first, to be "no."

For Jesus was a human being. He was born—male, and a Jew—to a woman named Mary, grew up in Nazareth of Galilee and, when he entered upon his career as preacher and healer, made the nearby town of Capernaum his headquarters. After what was, most likely, a brief ministry, he was arrested, during a Passover sojourn in Jerusalem, condemned as some kind of subversive, and executed (the Roman way) by crucifixion.

It is important to insist on Jesus' humanity for the sake not only of historical truthfulness but religious relevance. Certain passages in the New Testament can make Jesus sound almost like some extraterrestrial visitor, "coming down from heaven" and, after a time "here with us," "ascending into heaven" to be with God again.[10]

Such texts are helpful as ancient picture-language pointing to the belief that Jesus, crucified and risen, was and continues to be present to the God he called "Father" as well as to us whom (says the author of Hebrews) Jesus is "not ashamed to call . . . brothers and sisters."[11] But what must be insisted on is that in order to be our savior Jesus had to be like those "brothers and sisters"; had to be, in other words, fully and unmistakably human.

Human in his life, a life freely offered to God. And human in his death. Some early followers for whom Christ was simply a messenger from heaven bringing divine wisdom to our darkened minds found the harsh realism of the crucifixion story inconvenient. They insisted, therefore, on a "fake" death: either it was someone else who died—Jesus having escaped this trap—or this heavenly Jesus merely *seemed* to suffer on the cross.

To hold *only* to such a "no," however, would be to cut the heart out of the Christian faith. A "yes" has also to be spoken to the question about the divinity of Christ. But in making such an affirmation we would do well to avoid verbs like "is" and "was" ("Was Jesus God?") and find, instead, more dynamic, relational terms for stating this belief.

The Jesus recollected in all four Gospels is someone whose deeds and words—and even personal presence—could raise questions about links between the divine work of salvation and Jesus' ministry. His words were spoken, and his healing acts performed, with the kind of authority attributed to God's own self, rather than the delegated authority of a prophet or a scholar. Even more to the point, Jesus is remembered to have pronounced sins forgiven—thereby provoking experts in religion to ask indignantly (and tellingly), "Who can forgive sins but God alone?"[12]

The God talk would not have arisen, however, merely on the basis of what Jesus did and said. There was, after all, a death, marking the apparent utter failure of the Jesus project. If that had been the end, the Jesus story would have been about someone who died a martyr for what he understood to be the cause of God.

No, there had also to be that astonishing sequence of happenings spoken of, everywhere in the New Testament, as the "resurrection." In seeking to understand who Jesus was, what are we to make of the fact that the mission of Jesus did not after all fail, that even death could not eclipse that provocative, quickening presence?

The resurrection stories, however—the "appearances," the "empty tomb"—are not there so much to provide "proof" that "Jesus was God,"[13] as to convey meaning, the truth (again) that "in Christ God was reconciling the world to himself." What Jesus had done, what Jesus had said, the kind of God-imbued presence Jesus had been—even (and especially) the manner of Jesus' death—all were seen as having been divinely validated in what the followers spoke of as God's "raising Jesus from the dead." There took place, says William McClendon, a "re-identifying" of Jesus as the unique sharer of God's own identity, so that "for us, by this resurrection, the whole story of Jesus is God's own story."[14]

This "re-identifying" of Jesus in the "resurrection" can be discerned in certain *titles* that came to be associated, early on, with Jesus' role in God's saving work.[15] "Messiah," he was called (in Greek, "*Christos*"), meaning "anointed one," the one chosen ("anointed," like a king or high priest) for the fulfillment of God's promises to Israel and all humankind. "Son of God" also, suggesting the close relationship between God and and this one who spoke of God as "father."[16]

More importantly, Jesus came to be addressed and spoken of as "Lord." "Lord"—in Greek, *kyrios*—was the word used to convey one of the names of God in the Greek translation of Israel's Bible, the Septuagint. Furthermore, to address a Roman emperor as "*kyrios*" (Lord) would be to give divine status to that earthly ruler and to pledge not just political allegiance but quasi-religious worship. Anyone, then, voicing that Christian mini-creed "Jesus is Lord"[17] was declaring something like this: I worship God—the God of Israel and of all creation—through what puts me in touch with the spiritual reality of Jesus. I serve God according to the teachings of Jesus and in the power of the spirit of the risen Jesus. My highest loyalty is pledged not to any governing authority or any social-economic system but to God as known in Jesus.

That's what saying "yes" to the question "Was Jesus God?" really comes down to. But, someone will (justifiably) object, what about the language of the creeds in which we supposedly declare our belief in a Jesus who is "the only Son of God, eternally begotten of the Father . . . of one Being with the Father"?

The creeds were developed, during those early centuries of the Christian movement, to protect the foundational belief that the way God saves us has to do with Jesus. The conundrum the creed-makers wrestled with can be stated in an over-simplified but useful formula: Because only God can save, unless Jesus is (in some sense) God Jesus cannot *save* us. But, unless Jesus is fully identified with our humanness, Jesus cannot save *us*. And unless this allegedly saving personage is *both* human and divine, it cannot be *Jesus* who saves us. In resolving the puzzle, they made use of Scriptural stories, images, and concepts interpreted within thought patterns derived from Greek and Roman philosophy.

It is with the creedal formulas, then, as with the ancient images and ideas of Holy Scripture: They are of immense value; but if they are held to in literal terms, disregarding developments in intervening centuries, they can seriously mislead. It is because of fifth- and sixth-century language about the "two natures" of Christ, for instance, that some devout believers will speak (piously, but very misleadingly) of the "human part" of Jesus and the "divine part."[18]

Did Jesus have to die?

Anyone who watches sports events on TV is likely to have seen from time to time a sign held up containing the hand-lettered message: "John 3:16." The sign is meant to remind viewers of the divine offer of salvation as laid out in that verse from the Gospel of John—"God so loved the world that he gave his only Son, so that everyone who believes in him may not perish but may have eternal life."

Why did Jesus die? God (the sign-wavers would be saying) made it happen. The death was for our salvation. Only God can save. It had to have been God, therefore—so an influential strand of traditional reasoning would have it—who put Jesus on the cross.

That's partly because, within such a worldview, God is held to be directly responsible, in any case, for all that happens. Also because, in ancient religious practices, violations of the covenant with God were made right through the ceremonial slaughtering of animals. Jesus' death on the cross could be interpreted, then, as such a sacrificial offering. "Behold," says John the Baptist to a couple of his followers, with Jesus in view, "behold the lamb of God." In other words, whatever the sacrifice of an unblemished lamb had meant in the penitential system of Israel was now to be referred to Jesus and the divine desire to bring all humankind into right relationship through his death.[19]

What would Jesus have been doing on the cross, then? Representing us—according to this view—suffering the death due us as punishment for our sinful deeds. An acquaintance of mine used to declare, "Jesus took the bullet meant for me." God is just; sin must be punished; the ultimate penalty is death. But God is loving. And so Jesus was given for us, as our substitute, on our behalf. The crucifixion, then, would be a kind of transaction whereby God, by offering Jesus as a sacrifice, was satisfying some requirement within the divine reality having to do with the tension between mercy and justice.

Such thought patterns would seem to hover over the question "Did Jesus have to die?" And to that way of formulating a response the answer has to be "no." No, because of what it means to speak of Jesus as human. No, because of what it means to speak of God in relation to Jesus and all other human beings.

No, Jesus died as a human being, acting in freedom, and died at the hands of human beings acting in freedom. This was no puppet show, with a divine puppeteer working the strings. What happened outside Jerusalem two thousand years ago was what happens with heartbreaking predictability to all perceived as resisting any oppressive power elite. The "powers that be" take action to harass and humiliate, to silence—even, if necessary, to murder—anyone offering a vision of a new, liberating way of being.

But a "yes" can be affirmed, as well, in answer to the question "Did Jesus have to die?" If, that is, the "have to" is not about divine decree—God arbitrarily "deciding" that's the way things would be—but about divine character and consistency. And, at the same time, about human character and consistency. Why the physical outrage and soul's agony of Golgotha? Because humans were being what they tend to be: sinners resisting the divine vision. Because Jesus was being what he freely chose to be: the faithful "son." And because God was being what God eternally is, to all: love; holy love.

In these relational terms, the Jesus story would go something like this: Through Jesus' moment-by-moment wholehearted "yes" to divine promptings toward a certain way of being and a certain kind of mission, an unparalleled process of divine self-revealing was unfolding. "Long ago"—so begins the Letter to the Hebrews—"long ago God spoke to our ancestors in many and various ways by the prophets, but in these last days he has spoken to us by a Son."

But then, in the end, human sinfulness had its way with Jesus. His message was finally repudiated by those who felt its threat to their power and to their view of the world. These same leaders arranged to have him apprehended and tried, and cruelly put to death.[20] The powerless did what the powerless all too often do: nothing. At the site of the execution, so the story goes, some of the "the people" looked on passively while others let themselves be manipulated into shouting "Crucify, crucify him!" As for the ones who had been closest to Jesus, they scattered every which way and went into hiding.

The question is this: Given that God could obviously "use" for our salvation the exemplary life and healing work offered by Jesus, how could God make use of the ignominious failure of that mission and the agonizing death of that person? How is it that for followers of Jesus the profoundest symbol of divine salvation is the cross?

Did Jesus *have to* "rise from the dead"?

Jesus' death on the cross is not, by itself, a saving event. There has to be the resurrection. The dying is forever linked to the "rising again," the observance of Good Friday to the celebration of Easter Day. Must it be said, then, that in Jesus God "had to" triumph over death?

To the question as formulated a "no" must first be offered. Thinking about the resurrection, many envision a corpse stirring within a tomb, a stone rolling away from the opening, and a resuscitated body stepping out into a sunlit morning. But this image—of a resuscitation—can be very misleading.

For the stories are not about the "miraculous" coming-to-life of a corpse. They are about God's receiving into God's own eternal life all that the "Jesus event" had been—the wise, welcoming presence, the unfailing solidarity with those on the margins of their society, the liberating and reconciling deeds, the tranformative teaching, and the anguished death by crucifixion—and God's making that new life available, as the "spirit of the crucified-and-risen Jesus," to our realm of time and history.

The "appearances" in the four gospels, the "empty tomb" stories, Paul's "rollcall" (in 1 Corinthians chapter 15) of those to whom the risen Jesus was made manifest—are there to offer assurance of certain indispensable truths about the resurrection. Continuity, for one thing—in the disciples' conviction that the presence they became aware of from time to time after the death was "that same Jesus" with whom they had walked the hills of Galilee and the perilous streets of Jerusalem. Validation: the "reidentifying" of the life Jesus lived, and the cruel death Jesus died as embodying the depth of God's covenant partnership with humankind. God's ultimate overcoming, as well, of all that death means in human existence.

And the assurance of the availability of resurrection life for everyone, always: We who seek to follow Jesus now, at the beginning of the third millennium of the era so richly identified with his brief career in Palestine, have to do with the same wounded-and-glorified being spoken of as coming mysteriously into a gathering of fearful disciples and saying "Peace be with you" and breathing into them new life from God's Holy Spirit.[21]

By this time, clearly, the question heading this section is being answered with an emphatic "yes." But, once again, this "have to" is to be referred to God's "character," not to some arbitrary divine decree overriding all freedoms. Jesus' resurrection can be thought of, then, as the incomparable, luminous moment in which God was able, exercising divine freedom in relation to human freedom, to "give Jesus back" to the community of those faithful-fearful ones who, in the face of failure and peril, had fallen into despair. As the Apostle Peter testifies to the listening crowd on the Day of Pentecost, "This Jesus God raised up, and of that all of us are witnesses. Being therefore exalted at the right hand of God, and having received from the Father the promise of the Holy Spirit, he has poured out this that you both see and hear."[22]

What is being "poured out," New Testament "picture-thinking" tells us, is divine grace bringing salvation. It is from God, as salvation must always be. But the face of God therein discerned is, also, the face of Jesus—Jesus the healer and teacher from Galilee, Jesus the "suffering servant" of God and humankind in anguish on the cross, Jesus the "risen" presence in whom "death no longer has dominion."[23]

"Yes *and* no" to beliefs *about* Jesus; "Yes and I *don't* mean maybe!" to salvation *in* Jesus?

Once again, beliefs deriving from answers to the question *how* we can be saved through Jesus have to be held in a provisional "yes *and* no." What is it, though, that will enable us to offer—at the same time—faith's wholehearted "yes and I *don't* mean maybe" to the affirmation *that* "Jesus saves"? How is this tension between faith and belief to be maintained? By following, perhaps, the counsel of Michael Polanyi, who reminds us that, when confronted by mystery, we learn not by looking at the subject but by "dwelling in" it.[24] And by practicing, accordingly, those two interrelated disciplines of the spirit already mentioned: *immersion* and *identification*.

Immersion. Much of what this chapter has been doing so far is immersing us in the "old, old story of Jesus and his love." But what does identification entail? Placing ourselves in the story—what imaginative reader or hearer could fail to do so?—as fearful disciples, or faithful women from Galilee, or rough-and-ready soldiers, or scheming leaders, or uncomprehending onlookers. As Jesus himself—even, perhaps, in the moment when everything is called into question for him, including the trustworthiness of God.

And (dare it be said?) as God's own self. For the fact of the relationship between God and us invites us to enter with our hearts into what God might "feel": in the cries of the beloved victim, in the distress of the followers, in the nervous arrogance of those upholding the "domination system" and the stolid conformity of their brutalized functionaries, in the mindless thrill-seeking of the spectators—and in the unfathomable depths of God's own eternal wisdom and love.

The Emergence of Beliefs about Salvation through Jesus

Such immersion and identification was what was going on, in any case, among the first-century people learning to call themselves "Christians." As saving experience was reflected on and remembrances shared—and meanings searched for—beliefs began to take shape. Sources for hints as to meaning included, chiefly, the writings of ancient Israel which were for these believers "Scripture"—our "Old Testament"—and, secondarily, certain patterns of thought and practice from their Hellenistic cultural context.

What helpful images and symbols did these seekers find or create? Jesus the *sacrificial lamb*, for one thing, offered up in order to cleanse from sin and avert punishment due to fall on us. Jesus the *"servant"* of Second Isaiah,[25] whose sufferings in behalf of those estranged from God help bring about their restoration. Jesus the *redeemer*, the rescuer stepping in, at great cost, to "buy back" the freedom of those in thrall to debt or slavemasters. Jesus the *advocate*, pleading our seemingly hopeless case in the court of conscience before the "judge of all the earth," and securing our acquittal. Jesus our defenceless *defender* who by his death on the cross "disarmed the rulers and authorities" [what Walter Wink would speak of as "the powers"].[26] Jesus the *dying-rising god* of the Hellenistic "mystery religions" with whom we identify ourselves, in totality, so as to receive new being. Jesus the *"firstfruits* of those who have died," the beginning of the End, whose rising to new life in God was the first, and decisive, event in a saving sequence bringing all humankind to resurrection and all creation to its fulfillment under the eternal rule of God.[27]

We perceive in this process not a single supposedly correct understanding but great *diversity* of thought around a unifying center of conviction, inviting the kind of immersion and identification already spoken of. We note a *language* of faith rich with imagery, symbolism, and story—not necessarily to be read as descriptive, telling us what is "factually" the case, but (instead) as putting us in touch with spiritual truths beyond our grasp by invoking these realities in terms with which we are acquainted.

The context for such formulations, furthermore, is a *worldview* very different from ours, along with certain *religious practices* thoroughly foreign to us. We should expect to come at questions of belief from perspectives inherent in our"modern"—or "postmodern"—view of things, just as we should not be startled, in reading the old texts, to find such issues approached from one or another ancient worldview.[28] (Provided we keep in mind, as well, that our modern worldview, like each of those ancient ones, *is* only a "view," only a "perspective").

Rethinking Beliefs about Salvation through Jesus

Thinking about beliefs, though, is not a matter of simply saying "no" to older ways of thinking, anymore than it should entail, as fundamentalists might insist, merely surrendering with an uncritical "yes" to particular "frozen" interpretations of these great mysteries. It is a matter of "trying on" biblical story-shapes, image clusters, and structures of belief, with full awareness of problems posed for faith by ancient symbolic patterns and thought-forms while at the same time testing modern fragments of rethinking against formulations deriving from those earliest testimonies.

Coming at the "old, old story" this way, we find that the meaning of the event *is*, at the same time, its power to save. That's because through the immersion and identification of such seeking we *meet God* in the remembered Jesus. Meanings, here, do not consist in mere thought-about-at-a-distance interpretations; they draw us toward "I-*don't*-mean-maybe!" affirmations in which we can invest our lives. Faith does come, as Paul declares "by what is heard."[29]

And what do we learn, there at the cross? We learn about *sin*. Jesus "had to" die, it could be said, if human sinfulness was to come fully under judgment. Sin as our tuning out of the self-revealing presence; as our continual falling short of the glory that is ours as God's human creation; as our breaking of the rules by which we keep faith with the divine covenant partner and with our many "neighbors." And, in this new context, sin as that within us which is capable of putting someone like Jesus on something like a cross: sin as betrayal—giving over to destruction the person by whom one has been offered loyalty and love.

What do we learn? We learn about *Jesus*. Jesus "had to" die, as well, because of his own faithfulness. His was a resolve to remain "obedient to the point of death";[30] and it had to be based not on some supernatural knowledge that he would "come out of this alive," but on faith. Jesus could accept the likelihood that he would "have to" die if he could trust that the One who had called him to preach and enact the reign of God could bring saving possibilities even out of a last scene that threatened mere catastrophe.

The resolve of Jesus was grounded, even more deeply, in love—free, unforced love. When all had been done that could be done in resistance—non-violent resistance—to the powers of evil, there remained for Jesus the way of suffering love. Such suffering, empowered by divine grace, can expose the heinousness of what is being inflicted and, at the same time, convey a spirit of forgiveness toward those responsible.

For our learning at the cross is also about *God.* Jesus "had to" die, it must finally be said, because of the nature of the relationship between God and him. God participated fully in Jesus' thirty-or-so years. And "received" all that this life had been into God's eternal life. But if the freely-accepted *end* of that life can be seen as part of Jesus' act of self-giving, may we not say that God participated in, and thus received, the reality of that death? Is not our God, then, as the title of a book by German theologian Jurgen Moltmann asserts, a "crucified God"?[31] And would this not mean that the God who "gives" to us for our salvation the exemplary life offered by Jesus can also offer what is saving in the stark horror and seeming futility of that death?

Belief-metaphors like the altar of sacrifice, then, or the courtroom trial, or the buying-back of a debtor or a slave can bring home to us the costliness of salvation. If there is to be forgiveness and reconciliation—and release from sin's enslaving ways—a price must be paid, a kind of inner death must happen. Under judgment, whereby all that is misdirected and distorted in us is brought under the shadow of the cross, we learn the cost of our salvation—the cost to Jesus, the cost (in each moment of decision) to us, the cost, eternally, to God.

The image of the "*suffering servant*" brings to mind and heart the suffering on behalf of others evoked so tellingly in the images of Isaiah chapter 53 and seen by early believers in the Passion of Jesus. For those drawn into the divine love which permeates that self-offering and provides its center of meaning, such suffering has saving power.

As for the "*defenceless defender*" who on the cross "disarmed the rulers and authorities"—this image speaks to our longing for deliverance from the compulsion to avenge violence, to respond to force with force, to seek out scapegoats.[32] And its saving efficacy is witnessed to by the growing number of reforming efforts carried out by non-violent means and the soul-probing discipline of non-violent resistance.

All these avenues to salvation have presupposed *identification* with the saving reality of Jesus as crucified-and-risen and with God's participation in the totality of the Good Friday-Easter event. The Apostle Paul is our great exemplar here. "I have been crucified with Christ," he writes, "and it is no longer I who live, but it is Christ who lives in me. And the life I now live in the flesh I live by faith in the Son of God, who loved me and gave himself for me."[33] Sin is in our past. But as participants, through faith, in the history of Jesus, we can know ourselves, with respect to sin, as forgiven and, in principle, set free. Death is in our future. But so is the risen Jesus; and so, in Jesus, we can hold fast—as the poet Wordsworth assures us—to a "faith that looks through death" and cherish the hope that not even death "will be able to separate us from the love of God in Christ Jesus our Lord."[34]

A great twentieth-century Roman Catholic thinker, Karl Rahner, puts the case boldly. "Christianity is for me the simplest way," Rahner writes, "because it embodies the single totality of existence, plunges this totality calmly and hopefully with the dying Jesus into God's incomprehensibility and leaves all the details of life to us as they are, but without giving us a formula."[35]

Living Out our Faith in Salvation through Jesus

At the same time, identifying with God in the anguish and terror of the cross, we also identify with God's *triumph* over all that death can signify. Entering the darkness with the dying Jesus, we walk still in the light of God. "All of us who have been baptized in Christ Jesus" Paul declares, "were baptized into his death . . . so that, just as Christ was raised from the dead by the glory of the Father, so we too might walk in newness of life."[36]

"Newness of life": that is the keynote of salvation from God in Christ. "If anyone is in Christ, there is a new creation; everything old has passed away; see, everything has become new!"[37] And our response? Immerse ourselves in, and identify with, all that this means, in worship and in the life work Paul speaks of as the "ministry of reconciliation," whether close to home or among our farflung fellow-inhabitants of this "global village."

Where is the discipline of immersion and identification to be carried on? Everywhere, and anywhere. Part of what is indicated by the term "Holy Spirit" is that which has caused our society and culture to be pervaded with images of the one in whom "God was reconciling the world to himself" and inescapable questions about the meaning of Jesus as believed in around the world.

On the other hand, it is commonly understood that the place to go for the stories and sayings and images and beliefs concerning Jesus, and for practice in identifying with this crucified-and-risen one, is the church. The narrative about Jesus ascribed to Luke has a sequel by the same author; and that second book, the Acts of the Apostles, concerns the beginnings of what will be the topic of the next chapter: this "body of Christ" which is the church.

ENDNOTES

[1] Matthew 1:21.

[2] Matthew 1:22-23.

[3] John 14:6.

[4] Acts 4:12.

[5] Acts 10:34-35.

[6] Marjorie Hewitt Suchocki, *God—Christ—Church: A Practical Guide to Process Theology*, rev. ed. (New York: Crossroad, 1989), 176.

[7] Romans 1:16.

[8] Schubert Ogden, *The Reality of God and Other Essays* (San Francisco: Harper and Row, 1977), 173.

[9] Rowan Williams, *Resurrection: Interpreting the Easter Gospel* (Harrisburg, PA, Morehouse Pubishing, 1994), 71.

[10] John 3:13, e.g., and 6:32ff.

[11] Hebrews 2:17-18.

[12] Mark 2:7

[13] This is true also—though in a somewhat different way—of the motif of "virgin birth" (or "virginal conception") in the birth narratives of Matthew and Luke. What matters most in these story-metaphors is not Mary's alleged virginity but the action of God's Spirit. "The child conceived in her," the angel tells Joseph, her betrothed, "is from the Holy Spirit." It is not that belief in the divinity of Jesus derives from the story of a miraculous birth, but rather that the miraculous birth story derives from—and is a way of signalling—belief in the divinity, as well as humanity, of Jesus. See: Raymond E. Brown, S.S., *The Virginal Conception and Bodily Resurrection of Jesus* (New York: Paulist Press, 1973)

[14] James William McClendon, Jr., *Systematic Theology: Doctrine, Volume II* (Nashville: Abingdon Press, 1994), 247-48.

[15] A discussion of this development can be found in Raymond E. Brown, S.S., *An Introduction to New Testament Theology* (New York: Paulist Press, 1994).

[16] Once again, the masculine "father" does not speak of the gender of God but of the nature of the relationship between God and Jesus. As for the designation of Jesus as "son" and the fact that Jesus was male—these facts, likewise, have nothing to do with gender in God. Jesus the man became, in fact—receptive as he was of women along with men—a vehicle for reversing our valuation of genders. See: Suchocki, 99-101.

[17] 1 Corinthians 12:3, e.g.; 2 Corinthians 4:5; Philippians 2:11.

[18] A helpful account of the forming of the creeds is found in Frances Young, *The Making of the Creeds* (London: SCM Press and Philadelphia: Trinity Press International, 1991). Joan Chittister's *In Search of Belief* (Liguori, Missouri: Liguori/Triumph, 1999) provides a spirited restatement of the articles of the Apostles' Creed. See also Luke Timothy Johnson, *The Creed: What Christians Believe and Why It Matters* (New York: Doubleday, 2003).

[19] John 1:29. In the film *The Passion of the Christ*, produced (in 2004) by Hollywood star Mel Gibson, the physical suffering of Jesus is made so prominent (nine minutes elapsed time for the scourging!) that a sacrificial calculus seemed to be implied: the more blood shed, the more redemptive grace.

[20] Perhaps it still needs to be said, even after the public declarations of the Pope and of various other church leaders—that Christians must never interpret the story of the Passion in such a way as to carry forward the long-held, pernicious view that this death happened because these religious-political leaders were Jewish, that "the Jews killed Jesus." Gibson's *The Passion of the Christ*, already mentioned, seems, to many, to lean this way.

[21] John 20:19-22.

[22] Acts 2:33.
[23] Romans 6:9.
[24] Michael Polanyi, *Personal Knowledge* (New York: Harper and Row, 1964), x (in the preface to the Torchbook edition). "Understanding," Polanyi writes, "is based on our dwelling in the particulars of that which we comprehend." "Things which we can tell, we know by observing them; those that we cannot tell, we know by dwelling in them."
[25] "Second Isaiah" is the portion of Isaiah (chapters 40-55) usually ascribed to someone inspired by the original Isaiah but writing some one hundred fifty years after that prophet's time. The "servant hymns" are found in chapters 42, 49, 50, and 53.
[26] Colossians 2:15.
[27] 1 Corinthians 15:20.
[28] Certain ancient beliefs as to the saving value of Jesus' death on a cross are especially alien to a contemporary frame of reference. An imagined drama, for instance, in which a merciful Jesus intervenes with a righteous God in behalf of an otherwise doomed humanity—offering his death as compensation for human sin, or a "ransom" paid to the Devil, or "satisfaction" to a God whose honor (like that of a medieval lord) has been violated—is likely not to have meaning for many religious seekers today.

Various traditional understandings of the relation between Jesus' death and our salvation ("theories of the atonement") are helpfully discussed in Frances Young, *Can These Dry Bones Live? An Introduction to Christian Theology* (Cleveland: Pilgrim Press, 1993; originally pub. by SCM Press, 1982, 1992), chapters 2-5.
[29] Romans 10:17.
[30] Philippians 2:8.
[31] Jurgen Moltmann, *The Crucified God: The Cross of Christ as the Foundation and Criticism of Christian Theology*, trans. R. A. Wilson and John Bowden (Minneapolis: Fortress, 1993).
[32] The writings of René Girard—*Violence and the Sacred* (Baltimore: Johns Hopkins University Press, 1977), *The Scapegoat* (Baltimore: Johns Hopkins University Press, 1989), and other books—develop the relation between the death of Jesus and the human proclivity for scapegoating.
[33] Galatians 2:19-20.
[34] Romans 8:38-39.
[35] Karl Rahner, *The Practice of Faith: A Handbook of Contemporary Spirituality* (New York: Crossroad, 1983), 11.
[36] Romans 6:3-4.
[37] 2 Corinthians 5:17.

CHAPTER EIGHT

Can We be "Spiritual" without being "Religious"? Further Questions about God as Liberator and Reconciler

For those following the way of Christ there is no evading questions regarding the identity and role of the church. Even the fragmentary glimpses the New Testament provides, in the Acts of the Apostles and the "letters," make it clear that the church, as the "Body of Christ" continually breathed into life by the Spirit of that crucified-and-risen one, has been perceived from its inception to be a powerful, if problematic, force.

Many in these times, however, are unimpressed by claims on behalf of this spiritual-earthly body. Church worship is boring, they declare. Church attendance is uncool. Church people are inconsistent, even hypocritical. The church's beliefs are too narrow—or too broad; its positions on social-political issues are too conservative—or too radical. Ministers are always trying to tell you how to live, and then letting you down.

And anyway, as so many would now ask, who needs it? I can be "spiritual" without being "religious"—which, decoded, turns out to mean something like this: I have worked out my own individual practice for staying in touch with any "otherness" I may sense in my world, and I don't need to be part of a community of shared belief; specifically (and, often, especially!) that community known as the church.

Questions to be taken up in this chapter, then, include the following:

- *Can* we be "spiritual" without being "religious"?
- What *is* the "church"? And what does a church *do*?
- For certain questions can "yes-*and*-no" answers suffice—questions about religion and politics, for instance, or the church as "holy," or the church's ministers and ministry, or the alleged boringness of church worship?
- In the face of these "yes-*and*-no" answers, can we still also say "Yes and I *don't* mean maybe!" to the Church as divine gift?

Can we be "spiritual" without being "religious"?

In an important sense, everyone simply *is* spiritual. The quality of our attention to work and play, the mysterious aura around our individual being, the way we mourn, in advance, our eventual exit from life's stage—particular moments, as well, of speechless awe or erupting laughter or unbidden tears—these all mark us as "spiritual" creatures.

For to be "spiritual," once again, is simply to keep asking the questions that begin with "Why?" and seeking ways of honoring the dimensions of existence thus unveiled. The questioning happens in conversation or in "sessions of sweet silent thought." We practice meditation, perhaps, or traditional disciplines of prayer. We keep journals, attend workshops, read books on ways of focusing self-awareness and transfiguring ordinariness. But whether we take such special measures, or just "make do" with garden variety experiences of mystery and spasmodic attempts to pray, we are all "spiritual."

> A woman I know, in labor with her first child, answered the hospital admittance question about religious affiliation by indicating—in her desire to be scrupulously truthful—that she was not a church attender. Later, lying in her room mentally "singing psalms of praise" over the baby girl who had just been born and hearing (she would maintain) the music of angels, she looked down at her identification bracelet and caught the words "Religion: None"!

A "no" has to be offered, at the same time, to the question: "Can we be 'spiritual' without being 'religious'?" For even among those sincerely reaching toward God, a mainly individualistic approach to the mysteries of our created being can impoverish the relationship with God and one another.

Such a spirituality often fails to meet the needs of the *public sphere*. The books published by Robert Bellah and his team of sociologists on the general theme of "individualism and commitment in American life" make this point again and again. Privatized "faith," the authors insist, cannot supply a language warranting involvement in the needs of the larger community.[1]

Paradoxically, these researchers suggest, privatized spirituality provides a false picture of the *self*, as well. It causes us to forget that "we discover who we are face to face and side by side with others in work, love, and learning," in relationships, furthermore, "ordered by institutional structures and interpreted by cultural patterns of meaning."[2]

Someone, then, who asks, "Can I be 'spiritual' without being 'religious'?" may even be *formulating* the question wrongly. Is it enough to decide, "*I* don't need the church"? Isn't there a further question: "Do others need *me* to be a part of the church?" "I had a voice," Saul Bellow's Henderson declares, "that said, I want!" But then comes a new realization: "*I* want? I? It should have told me *she* wants, *he* wants, *they* want."[3]

As to those for whom "spirituality" means intentional exploration of our connections with God as the "presence to which all reality is present," earlier chapters have already made something of a case for this community of faith that is the church.

The God who is self-revealing mystery is sensed in the signs of that presence. But such signs are read in light of Holy Scripture, and interpreting those biblical texts is a task assigned to the community of believers. If "a good religion resembles a language," as suggested in the Howatch novel quoted earlier, it makes sense, if one wishes to "gain fluency [in this language], . . . to go where the language [is] regularly spoken."[4]

The concerted endeavors in the public sphere advocated in the Robert Bellah books are to be taken on with special urgency by those called to work—in the language of Chapter Three—as co-creators and co-preservers with God. And such obligations are indispensable to the work of Christ's church.

How do we "keep covenant"with God? Chapter Four inquired. Part of the answer was "observance." We seek to express wholehearted love for God in the offering of thanksgiving and praise, the discipline of prayer, and the intentional listening for "a word from God" that constitute a congregation's worship.

In the chapters on salvation, the church figured large as the place where we learn to claim our liberation and reconciliation, immersing ourselves in all that has to do with Jesus and identifying ourselves, more and more, with that crucified-and-risen one made present through the Spirit.

The Letter to the Hebrews, then, rightly urges its readers to "provoke one another to love and good deeds," while at the same time "not neglecting to meet together."[5] For if we are to flower into personhood, fulfill our vocation as co-creators with God, live up to what is asked of us as citizens of our nation and of the world, and welcome the fullness of divine salvation, we will require something other than a privatized spirituality.

What *is* the Church? What does a church *do*?

> I myself have been a late learner about church. In reaction against an over-churched childhood and youth, I spent a good part of middle life as a non-attender, settling into my Sunday morning ritual of newspapers and coffee, successfully resisting the occasional impulse to return.
>
> There was no sense, though, of having repudiated Christian faith itself. And I continued, through various personal practices, to be a "spiritual" person.
>
> Suddenly, one day in early 1980, at a moment of shared grief and personal crisis, I knew I had to be a churchgoer again. This time the impulse came as a firm resolve, the resolve was carried out the very next Sunday, and the decision about one Sunday turned into a consistent week-by-week, year-by-year practice.

As one who has "looked at church from both sides now" (to paraphrase a song of the Sixties), what have I, on reentry, found the church to be? Much of what it was meant to be, according to the witness of the New Testament—though in many ways (the usual ways!) falling short, also, of that intention.

What the Church Is*—A Certain Kind of Community*

Over against the individualistic spirituality described earlier, the church is called to be a *community* . To be in the church is to be a member of a body, both a local group—a parish, a church, a "fellowship" of some sort—and the assembly, worldwide, of all who gather "in the name of Jesus."

With few exceptions, this community does not, however, live apart, unto itself. It *participates* in the work of its society, sharing the anguish and the exaltation, and the day-to-day ordinariness, of its particular place and time.

What kind of community is it, then? Not an affinity group, like-minded people pursuing common interests. Nor a task-oriented group like a committee or board. Not even, mainly, an organization (as in the "organized religion" about which dismissive things are so often said). The church—in the language of the Apostle Paul—is the *"body of Christ."*[6] This band of people is brought together by a shared faith in God as decisively present in Jesus the Christ and a shared belief that the power of salvation present then, in that teacher and healer from Galilee, is with us now in the Spirit of the crucified and resurrected Christ.

What does the church claim as its purpose, its goal? Something outside itself. Not simply its continuance as church, but the fulfillment of a *calling*. This calling—the one Jesus himself embraced and embodied—is to proclaim and enact the "reign of God" in the world.

The shape of the church's life, accordingly, is the figure inscribed by the life of Jesus. In modeling divine wisdom and carrying out Christlike works of love, its members will need to "sign on" to the terms for discipleship so clearly laid down in Mark chapter 8, where Jesus is remembered as saying: "If any want to become my followers, let them deny themselves and take up their cross and follow me." Terms set out also in Paul's words reminding us that we were "buried with [Christ] by baptism into death, so that, just as Christ was raised from the dead by the glory of the Father, so we too might walk in newness of life."[7]

"Newness of life." Yes. For every church body is also (in Rowan Williams' phrase) a "community of resurrection."[8] Its message proclaims, its pattern of existence can embody, authentic hope for the recurrent newness promised to all who identify with the dying of Christ. In the words of a contemporary hymn, by Fred Pratt Green,

> The church of Christ in every age,
> beset by change but spirit led,
> must claim and test its heritage
> and keep on rising from the dead.[9]

What the Church **Does:** *Welcoming, Worshiping, Making Disciples, Serving the World*

As a community centered in Jesus Christ, dedicated to furthering the reign of God, existing according to the pattern offered by the life and death and resurrection of Christ, what is it that the church, when true to itself, characteristically does?

First, it *welcomes* all who wish to participate in its life. Following the example of that welcoming Christ, the church, by its very nature, is inclusive. It makes its "good news" known (in the words of the Roman Catholic writer Richard Rohr), to

> youth who want both inspiration and structure, feminists who must know that they have an essential truth, patriarchs who need to be challenged but not dismissed, . . . the broken who don't need more words

> but a healing touch, the seekers who need depth and patience, . . . gays and lesbians who need acceptance before agenda, males who need soul work, parents who need skills, the oppressed who need justice and solidarity, believers who need to believe again.[10]

In most faith communities, seekers ready to affirm the "God and Father of our Lord Jesus Christ" as the ultimate object of their search are welcomed in a particular symbolic action, the rite of initiation known as Baptism. Upon their response in faith[11] to the words affirming the saving grace of God in Christ and the water applied as sign of cleansing and new life, those baptized are invited to participate in the community's life together, its service to the world, and its maintenance of its own order.

As a community, secondly, the church *worships*. It devotes itself, like the converts we read about in Acts chapter 2, to "the apostles' teaching and fellowship, to the breaking of bread and the prayers."[12] It thus acknowledges and celebrates the divine life it continually receives, the identity to which it aspires, the calling it seeks to fulfill, and the eternal promise in which it rests.

Along with praise and prayers offered and truth proclaimed, worship in almost all church bodies also provides for a ritual making-present of the crucified and resurrected Christ through the sharing of bread and wine. This action is identified, variously, as the Lord's Supper (since the institution of this ritual meal is attributed to Jesus himself), or Holy Eucharist (from the Greek word for "thanksgiving"), or Holy Communion, or the Mass (from a word in the Latin liturgy used for centuries by the Roman church), or (in Eastern Orthodox usage) the Divine Liturgy. Churches differ considerably in their understanding of the meaning and the importance of this symbolic (or, for many, "sacramental") meal.[13]

Attempts may be made, as well, to incorporate recognition of the sacred in the ways we mark specific times and transitions in time. Sunday itself, remembered as the "day of resurrection," is almost everywhere the "Lord's Day" set aside for the principal services of worship. The "historic signs" of the Christian faith are given special recognition at Christmas and Good Friday and Easter and Pentecost. In some traditions, the story of salvation is symbolically called to mind by the marking off of the calendar year into seasons of "sacred time" constituting a "liturgical year." A marriage can be "blessed" and celebrated in a "church wedding." A person of faith who has died is remembered before God in prayer and commended to the divine mercy, in a funeral service.

The church is also a community called to "*make disciples*."[14]—not just a rest area for weary travelers but also a training center for world-transforming effort. It provides means, therefore, by which its members can learn (in the words of an old formulation) to "pray the prayer of Christ, learn the mind of Christ, and do the deeds of Christ."[15]

Besides the opportunities for worship already mentioned, such means include: first, encouragement of individual spiritual practice whereby one can better "pray the prayer of Christ." The Church, after all, offers a rich tradition of solitary meditation and prayer, our teachers ranging from fourth-century "Desert Fathers" (and Mothers) to spiritual masters of our own time It also welcomes numerous spiritual practices from other traditions of meditation and prayer.

Second, group and individual study for "learning the mind of Christ." For the church is a learning community, as well, one in which children and adults of the church "family" hear about, talk over, and try out in their lives the great stories and images and sayings and beliefs which are our heritage. To say that the church is "apostolic" is, partly, to affirm that it remains rooted in the originating texts to which it traces its very being, even while staying open also to that guiding Spirit who is continually "making all things new."[16]

Training, finally, in "doing the deeds of Christ." Members of a church are to work together, as a community called to *serve*—to serve one another in the "body" and to serve the needs of a world which God creates and for which Christ died and rose again. Those following Jesus in the way of the cross share a mission to the world, one which came originally (according to our Gopels) in the form of a *commission* from Jesus himself.

As a community of faith celebrating the presence of Christ, the church is intended to model the actualizing of God's rule. Its prayer ("Thy kingdom come, thy will be done . . .") is to be integrated with its action "on earth." The test for any spiritual movement, says theologian Kenneth Leech, is the degree to which it "has enabled us to see with greater penetration and insight into the roots of the world's pain . . . [and] to respond more dynamically and more effectively to that pain."[17]

In its own ongoing activities, the church, as a house of welcome, should cherish the unique personhood and the particular gifts of each of its members. It should encourage free and full participation, according to the nature of those gifts, in its worship, its process of "discipling," and its ordering for leadership. And it should be known, above all, as a center of caring, forgiving love, with a minimum of bickering and backbiting, of smoldering resentments, of competitiveness and jealousy.

At the same time, the church's specific mission is to bring a message, to proclaim the good news of salvation from God in Jesus. How? Not by way of the confrontational, even coercive, approach stereotypically associated with the church, even yet, by some of those outside looking in but through the offering of a gracious invitation to those "with ears to hear" and a willingness to enter into heart-probing conversation about what God continually offers a humanity alienated and enslaved through sin. Those saying "yes" to the invitation become, in turn, members of the church and take part in all that has been described in relation to what the church is and does.

What about the questions to which the answer has to be "Yes *and* no"?

To the picture just presented some with disillusioning experience might be ready to reply: "In your dreams!" And in a sense they would be right: What has been sketched in previous pages *is* a dream—not a series of snapshots of the church making its very uneven way through the twenty centuries of its history so far, but a *vision* of the church being and doing all that is expected of it.

Questions precipitated by the mingledness of that history must be confronted. These are questions to which, at best, "yes-*and*-no" answers can be given. But, again, such two-sided answers must not preclude a faithful response—a strong "yes and I *don't* mean maybe!"—to the church itself as divine gift and calling.

Of the many questions that come to mind—some having been taken up in passing in earlier chapters—four will receive space for slightly more extensive consideration: questions about the quality of the church's worship services, the "holiness" of its members, the status of its "ministers," and the church's stance toward political issues.

Can we expect worship services to be pleasurable?

No, worship is not pleasure. At least, not if pleasure is equated—as it tends to be in our time—with entertainment. For one thing, those who worship are not an "audience" but participants, contributing therefore to the quality of the worship that is offered. And gifts vary. Hymns are scheduled, but the voices present to sing them may be weak. Accompanists may have had insufficient training. Those doing the Scripture readings may not be experienced in reading aloud in public. Some preachers are not as gifted as others in preparing sermons or presenting them.

But, more to the point, worship is not *about* entertainment. As worshipers we are asked to throw off expectations of being entertained or distracted and to know ourselves, instead, as making an offering—"a sacrifice" (in the words, once again, of Hebrews) "of praise to God, . . . the fruit of lips that confess [God's] name."[18]

But that model of worship as a self-offering to God, an ordered, communal response to divine presence, does enable a "yes" to our question. For such intention assures the kind of attention that can infuse a church's prayer and praise with pleasurableness as well as meaning. Attention given, for one thing, to preparations for the service—to words read and spoken, music and movement, setting and accoutrements— so that such elements are not thoughtlessly put together or conducted in a slipshod manner.

Attention, even more, on the part of the worshipers themselves. For whenever that kind of attentiveness is present—the dedicated concentration required for performing in public, let's say, or perfecting a golf swing, or listening to a beloved voice—everything about the worship experience is transformed.

> For some weeks after the return to church spoken of earlier, I found all the elements of the liturgy haloed, the words reverberating within me. In time, of course, there was a diminishing of "the glory and the dream." But that "high" has returned, on numerous occasions—when attention opened the door for it—and I have come to expect, from each Sunday's self-offering in worship, something that is neither ecstasy nor boredom but a steady, deepening joy.

Is the membership of a church made up of holy people?

The answer has first to be, defiantly: yes. Yes, the Creed is correct in affirming "one *holy* catholic and apostolic Church." But, as was suggested earlier, this is a *derived* holiness, part of the gift of covenant relationship with God in Christ. It is the holiness of God we are talking about here. When we gather, from Paul's letters, what was going on among the believers at Corinth, it seems almost laughable that they should be addressed as "holy ones" ("saints"). But they were indeed "saints"—and so are we who share their trust in divine forgiveness and seek to position ourselves within that same energy field of divine holiness.

For that "Spirit of holiness" can also enliven and remake us. Words from the Apostle Paul promise that if we will "present [our] bodies as a living sacrifice, holy and acceptable to God, which is [our] spiritual worship," we will be "transformed by the renewing of [our] minds . . . ."[19]

People who station themselves in the region of the holy will themselves be empowered to manifest the same marks of holiness—personal integrity in being and doing, compassion and yearning for justice in relation to others—that are attributed to *God* when God is spoken of as "holy."

The need for a "no" answer is equally obvious. Believers remain sinners, even as they earnestly seek to accept saving grace. In our freedom we give way to attitudes and behaviors contrary to the spirit of Christ and, therefore, hurtful to others and to ourselves. The more this happens, the more a contrary spirit can move in, diminishing a church's vitality, corrupting its activities, and damaging the reputation of the church itself and the Christ it represents.

At such times, the church's members have access to a precious secret regarding holiness. The secret is not about achieving perfection but about dealing with imperfection. It is the way of confession and forgiveness. "If we say that we have no sin," the First Letter of John tells us, "we deceive ourselves." But, the passage continues, "if we confess our sins, he who is faithful and just will forgive us our sins and cleanse us from all unrighteousness."[20]

Here, a sub-question comes to mind as well: Should the church try to tell *you and me* how to be "holy"? Some people picture ministers of churches—and members, also—as keeping them under a kind of moral surveillance, to make sure they are not "being bad." And putting them through instruction, at the same time, on how to "be good"—largely by way of a list of things we are *not* supposed to do.

To such moralism we must learn to say "no." Holiness, it was said earlier, comes to characterize our lives as we stay connected to a God who is holy. Just being *told* what is right or wrong for us won't bring that outcome. The way the church *can* help us is mainly by directing us to those practices, traditionally called the "means of grace," whereby we can seek to remain open to the promptings of the Spirit of God. And by providing us, as well, with a "safe" place to explore issues related to our aspirations for "holy living." An awareness of being watched, a sense of being held guilty until proven innocent—these are just what the "doctor" (the divine diagnostician and healer) has *not* ordered!

But this means that an indirect "yes" has also found its way into the response. One of the means of grace by which we "learn the mind of Christ" is acquaintance with the profound wisdom in Holy Scripture. In this sense, the church *can* be "telling us" something of what is required for holy living, that lifelong project whereby we are "transformed into the . . . image [of Christ], from one degree of glory to another."[21]

Could it be said that the quality of a church's life depends on its **minister?**

"Oh, our church is doing so well," a churchperson will say; "we have such a good minister." "Why should I go to church?" says someone who "never darkens the door." "Look at the way your ministers behave!" Each of these remarks implies a "yes" response to the question heading this section, but these poles-apart "yeses" also evince a flawed understanding both of ministry and of those popularly spoken of as "ministers."

Yes, whenever something goes scandalously wrong in some church body, when boundaries have been transgressed, rules broken, vulnerable people (even children!) exploited, it will almost always be one or another "Father" or "Reverend," or "Pastor" that is spotlighted. And yet, there is really no reason to be surprised by such happenings. Everybody receiving salvation from God in Christ remains, at the same time, susceptible to temptation. Those with the honorific titles conferred by the church are no exceptions!

Special coverage for the shenanigans of the "Revs," special commendations for their good work—both derive from a mistaken idea of ministry itself. The point was made earlier that the calling shared by all followers of Jesus is that of service, service to one another and service ("ministering") to the world God wants to sustain and befriend and save. All ministers in the church are servants, and all who serve the church are "ministers."

The man or woman conventionally spoken of as the "minister," therefore—or pastor, or priest—is essentially one among a number of people serving a particular church, all of whom are commissioned to the task by virtue of their baptism. The gifts of the Spirit whereby the church is to be served, according to Ephesians, are poured out "to equip the saints [meaning all members] for the *work of ministry*."[22]

The service of pastor usually requires a high degree of preparation, however, and involves special forms of leadership. It ordinarily entails being ordained (and becoming a "Reverend"). And so it is easy for others who serve less visibly and with less authority conferred on them to give special value to this work and even to put such a minister on, so to speak, a pedestal.

Thereby arises much of the trouble." Hoisted onto that pedestal, carrying a title like "the Reverend Ms. or Mr. or Dr.," it is easy to forget the truth Jesus made so clear to the ministers-in-training who were his disciples that the leader among them must be "like one who serves."[23]

On that "pedestal," one can be especially vulnerable, as well, to lurking temptation. Complacency sets in. Awareness of besetting sin is stifled. Resources for self-examination are neglected. And soon come the troubles in the congregation: the smoldering resentments and sudden eruptions, the subtler encroaching of indifference to worship and witness. And, all too often (with great publicity!), the scandals—about the fast-and-loose handling of church funds, the concealed adulterous affair, the long-unacknowledged sexual abuse of children and youth.

"Yes *and* no," then, to the question heading this section. Yes, because a pastor—representing the holy, loving God revealed in Jesus Christ—carries much responsibility and can, therefore, cause much harm. But no, since "ministry" is carried on by all the people, not just the person with the title. And once again, yes, in view of that truth. Yes (changing the form of one word in the question), "the quality of a church's life does depend on those (meaning *all* members) who are its "ministers."

Should the church "be involved in politics"?

The "yes" part of a short answer to the question about the church's involvement with politics would go something like this: The church should not—indeed, cannot—"stay out of politics." Simply to be human is to engage in political activity. The work of the Spirit for the furtherance of God's reign can be discerned in many movements and individual leaders that have nothing to do with church or with religion as such. "Separation of church and state," then, is not equivalent to a separation of religion from politics. And so individual church members, and entire church bodies, will advocate for—and encourage serious discussion of—certain policies considered to have bearing on the divine intention for a particular community, an entire nation, or the whole world.[24]

But also: No. Care needs to be taken to keep churches from strictly *partisan* political ties. Christians must always reserve their full allegiance for something beyond party—or, for that matter, nation. Such distancing enables a church body to bring prophetic criticism to bear on any political faction, while supporting whatever policy (and whatever party) appears to be the best on offer at any given time.

People of faith will also dissociate themselves from policies proposed merely to enhance the power or status of the church itself as an institution. Or to impose its values, inappropriately—by way of manger scenes in town centers, for example, the Ten Commandments posted on courtroom walls, or public prayer in classrooms or at school games—on what has now become a pluralistic society.

"Yes *and* no" to the questions—but also, "Yes and I *don't* mean maybe!" to the church?

Is participation in the life of the church required of us who follow the way of Christ? For family people, is it worthwhile to keep saying, "Yes, and I *don't* mean maybe!" to the trouble of getting themselves and the kids ready on Sunday mornings? Does it make sense for a sophisticated single person, week after week, to be involved with something this "uncool," or for a long-retired older man or woman to brave bad weather or aching joints to keep up the old churchgoing habit?

If it *is* required, if it is worthwhile, then what is needed is a yes-and-I-*don't*-mean-maybe! commitment. This would entail an embracing, first of all, of the *vision* presented here of what the church can be, along with realistic expectations in view of the undeniably mingled results of past efforts by this saintly-yet-sinful body.

A proactive rather than reactive stance, as well: a resolve to *be* that envisioned reality, as much as possible, rather than be half-player-half-spectator waiting for fellow churchgoers, and/or the church's pastor, to measure up to standards for holiness and hospitality set by us sitting in judgment.

Which means a week-after-week involvement, not just occasional drop-ins. In a way, churchgoing is like taking antibiotics: one capsule won't do it, the whole "course" is called for. What church provides—to change images—is not a glaze but a marinade.[25]

As those committed to the church, we take on the task, as well, of making our witness—not in an overbearing manner but with the humility of "one who serves," seeking to invite and persuade rather than coerce, as befits God's way of relating to all of us in freedom. A famous painting depicts the scene imaged in Revelation in which Christ says (to the church at Laodicea), "Listen! I am standing at the door knocking; if you hear my voice and open the door, I will come in to you and eat with you, and you with me."[26] Looking closely at the painting, one realizes that this door at which the Savior is knocking can be opened only from the inside.

The question, then, is not really "Can I be 'spiritual' without being 'religious'?" The "without" is inadmissible. The question has to be: "How can I be spiritual *and* religious?" The answer encompasses joining with others in community for worship, for listening and interchange, and for sharing in "works of love," while maintaining what one finds doable by way of an individual spiritual practice of prayer, meditation, study and reflection. Only when our "religion" and our "spirituality" are thus made one can we fully enter into the vision of Jesus, which is also the goal of the Church: "[God's] will . . . done on earth as it is in heaven."

In a brief autobiographical piece about her refinding of the Christian heritage, writer Kathleen Norris explains, giving reasons both humorous and serious, why she is now a churchgoer. "It's the one place I know," she writes,

> where I am allowed to sing in public, no matter what my voice sounds like, and where I receive a blessing just for showing up. Even more important, it is a place set aside from the noise and relentless commerce of the world for giving thanks for all that is larger than myself. I can join a ragtag band of other people and praise the God who made and sustains us, and who every week renews our hope that a loving and creative spirit is at work in us, and in the whole creation. Like nothing else I know, it brings me back to my senses.[27]

ENDNOTES

[1] Robert Bellah et al., *Habits of the Heart: Individualism and Commitment in American Life* (Berkeley and Los Angeles: University of California Press, 1985); *The Good Society* (New York: Alfred A. Knopf, 1991).

[2] Bellah, *Habits of the Heart*, 84.

[3] Saul Bellow, *Henderson the Rain King* (Harmondsworth, Middlesex, England: Penguin Books, 1959), 286.

[4] Susan Howatch, *Absolute Truths* (New York, Alfred A. Knopf, 1995), 271.

[5] Hebrews 10:24-25.

[6] Romans 12:4-5; 1 Corinthians 12:27; Ephesians 4:15-16.

[7] References are to Mark 8:35-35; Romans 6:3-4.

[8] Rowan Williams, *Resurrection: Interpreting the Easter Gospel* (Harrisburg, PA, Morehouse Pubishing, 1994), title of Chapter 3.

[9] F. Pratt Green, "The church of Christ in every age," in *Wonder, Love, and Praise: A Supplement to The Hymnal 1982* (New York: Church Publishing Inc., 1997), number 779.

[10] Richard Rohr, O.F.M., "Holy Fools," *Sojourners* (July, 1994), 20.

[11] Many church groups baptize only persons capable of making such a "profession of faith" on their own. There is, however, a "catholic" tradition of baptizing infants or children, with parents and congregation making promises on behalf of the one baptized and agreeing to "support this person in his or her life in Christ"—in the expectation, as well, of an individual commitment at a later time. A good summary of agreements and disagreements among major church bodies on beliefs regarding Baptism can be found in *Baptism, Eucharist, and Ministry*. Faith and Order Paper No. 111 (World Council of Churches, Geneva, 1982), 2-7.

[12] Acts 2:41-42.

[13] Further discussion of such differences of belief and practice among church bodies

must be omitted here in order not to transgress the necessarily limited scope of this book. Summary statements of beliefs regarding Eucharist appear in *Baptism, Eucharist, and Ministry*, 10-17.

[14] Matthew 28:19-20.

[15] Source unknown; mission statement, for some years, of the Episcopal Diocese of Vermont.

[16] Revelation 21:5.

[17] Kenneth Leech, *Experiencing God: Theology as Spirituality* (San Francisco: Harper and Row, 1985), 347.

[18] Hebrews 13:15.

[19] Romans 12:1-2.

[20] 1 John 1:8-9.

[21] 2 Corinthians 3:18.

[22] Ephesians 4:11-12.

[23] Luke 22:25-27.

[24] Helpful suggestions for dealing with political issues in a congregational setting are found in Brian McLaren's "Risky Business," *Sojourners* (September 2004), 14-18.

[25] The words are those of Urban T. Holmes III, in *What Is Anglicanism?* (Wilton, CT: Morehouse-Barlow, 1982), 61.

[26] Revelation 3:20.

[27] Kathleen Norris, "Waiting for Dakota: Looking for God in the Wrong Places," *Modern Maturity* (March/April 2001), 38.

CHAPTER NINE

Are Heaven and Hell Real? And Other Questions about God as Source and Hope of Eternal Life

The words, of course, are on everybody's lips—"heaven," "hell," "end of the world"—whether in jokes about St. Peter and the pearly gates or metaphoric tags in old songs ("Heaven: I'm in heav-en . . . when we're out together dancing cheek to cheek"). Or more directly, through our increased familiarity—after Y2K and the best-selling "Left Behind" series—with such biblical motifs as "the Millennium," "the Rapture," and "the New Jerusalem."

Behind all this, however, lurks a profound uncertainty as to what realities, if any, might be intimated by ancient, freighted words like "a better world" or "the resurrection of the dead, and the life everlasting," or—praying the Lord's Prayer—"thy kingdom come."

Among the many questions that could be entertained on such matters the ones chosen for this chapter include the following:

- Is there "life after death"? In what mode: Resurrection? "Immortality"?
- Are heaven and hell real? "Purgatory"? How would one "get to heaven"? Could anyone be thought of as "going to hell"?
- Will the world "come to an end"? And what could be meant by such biblical symbols as Kingdom of God? Second Coming? the Judgment?
- If such questions have to be answered "yes *and* no," can we nevertheless offer a "yes and I *don't* mean maybe!" to God as source and hope of eternal life?

What assumptions should undergird our thinking about "last things"?

With regard to questions like these, differences of worldview really matter; and presuppositions, therefore, need to be set forth.

First, it must be remembered that this is all about *God*. Every doctrine—including teaching about Hell—said 19th-century theologian F. D. Maurice, is meant as a pointer to God, and not as a colorful description of a counterpart world.[1] The God thus pointed to is one fully in relationship with humankind and all creation. And the character of this relationship is most adequately revealed in the crucified and risen Jesus.

To be in relationship with God, though, is to know that all we feel and do finds its ultimate home in that creative, just, loving presence. "In your unchanging eternity," St. Augustine wrote, in that extended prayer called the *Confessions*, "you are preparing a barn for the harvest of our fleeting years."[2] Whatever else the word might encompass, "heaven" would have to mean life, eternal life, with God. "Hell" would have to be about separation from God. The accomplished reign of God—God's realized "kingdom"—would be the fulfillment of the prayer so often uttered: "Thy will be done, on earth as it is in heaven."

It must be assumed, secondly, that our individual lives, and the multifarious "lives" encompassed in the term "history," can be imaged as "*story*." Out of the mingled freedoms and unfreedoms of the world's happenings patterns take shape, meanings emerge—all related, ultimately, to the supreme figure in the story. And so each little story within God's greater story will include a beginning, a "plot" constructed out of personal decisions, social-political-economic forces, and chance happenings, and, as well, some sort of ending.

But is that "ending" *the* end? God, the protagonist of the all-encompassing story, is spoken of as "eternal." Dare we say what the narrative voice declares, in the concluding sentence of *The Last Battle* (the final volume in C. S. Lewis's Narnia series), that with the death bringing some life story to an end begins "Chapter One of the Great Story, which no one on earth has read: which goes on for ever: in which every chapter is better than the one before"?[3]

Such questions suggest a third assumption: namely, that the ultimate issue here is *death*. Death is one "last thing" all believe in, an "end of the world" everyone can expect to undergo. We fear our own dying and the loss of those beloved by us. We can even envision, with Shakespeare's Prospero, a de-creating moment in which "the great globe itself, / Yea, all which it inherit, shall dissolve, / And . . . leave not a rack behind"[4]

The word "envision" points toward yet another presupposition for talk of "last things": The *language* will be that of image, symbol, metaphor, vision. For this is the realm of mystery: the mystery of the divine reality, already spoken of in earlier chapters; the mystery of our human way of being; and now, the incomprehensibility of "that undiscovered country from whose bourn," as Hamlet reminds us, "no traveler returns."

Biblical teaching about death, heaven, hell, and the kingdom of God comes to us mostly, as theologian James McClendon points out, by way of "picture-thinking."[5] Whoever reads Holy Scripture with these themes in mind—or later writings influenced by the Bible, for that matter—is confronted with a fascinating collage of visionary images: a "fiery chariot" which "swings low" to carry a prophet "home"; a peaceable kingdom where "the wolf shall live with the lamb"; a "Son of Man . . . coming on the clouds of heaven"; a gigantic Satan frozen eternally in the lowest depths of the "Inferno"; a "holy city, the new Jerusalem," in which "death will be no more" and all tears shall be wiped away."[6]

For those to whom questions about death and "life after death" are of intense concern, this biblical picture-language can lead down deceptive interpretive passageways.[7] To urge a literal reading of the symbol of hellfire, to narrate a bloody massacre visited by Jesus on the Antichrist's unbelieving armies, to picture believers in Christ as being actually "taken up into heaven" while those not subscribing to Christian beliefs are "left behind"—all this is to misconstrue the sacred writings, mislead people of faith, and misrepresent the relationship between God and the creatures to whom God gives life and offers salvation.

At the same time, as McClendon rightly insists, "picture-thinking" must be taken seriously; for it can be "governed by a depiction of the end toward which everything tends," and its words can *evoke* realities they cannot fully represent.[8] The task here, as always, is one of responding to such texts with a ready "yes" to the God they make present and with an equally ready "yes *and* no" to certain interpretations of what we find there.

Belief questions like these, though—more so than those considered in earlier chapters—may also permit of a few "and-I-*do*-mean-maybes." In full awareness of the dangers incurred in entering the realm of "maybe"-as-speculation, the thought-journey now to be entered upon will include several such excursions.

Is there "life after death"?

We start with the question closest to home: "Is there 'life after death'? Our response has first to be a kind of "*no*." No, when we die, we really die; we do not "live on," simply changing horses, as it were, and then riding on.[9] Biblical writers, by and large, do not affirm a split such that only the physical component of a person dies while an "immortal soul" survives. For them, dead means dead; and certain psalms pointedly remind God that from those who are in the shadowy realm called Sheol no offerings of worship and praise can be expected.[10]

The possibility of a biblical "*yes*" to the question heading this section emerged together with a belief in resurrection, which developed late among the writings of the Old Testament[11] and which, because of belief in Jesus' resurrection, became central to the faith of the early church.

New Testament writings are suffused with the joy and hope believers in Jesus derived from the word that "God has raised Jesus from the dead." Joy, because this means that always God will be present to them as the Spirit of the one who "was dead . . . [and is] alive for ever and ever."[12] A living hope, because, according to the teaching of the Apostle Paul, to be in that reconciling, liberating presence now, through faith, is also to participate then—when the final fear is upon us—in Christ's triumph over death.[13]

Then there are the sub-questions—largely questions about "how"—all of which call for something of a "*maybe*" response. How is it that we are "raised up" by God? "Maybe" answers in Holy Scripture include: corpses coming out of their burial places in reconstituted bodies, believers "raptured" from their graves to "meet the Lord in the air," and dead persons simply finding themselves "away from the body and at home with the Lord."[14]

Theologian Marjorie Suchocki suggests that such images and story-fragments are ways of saying that God receives us, at our death—for judgment and for transformation—into God's own eternal life. Receives the "finished project," so to speak: the sum total of all that has been felt, thought, suffered, and enacted within the years that have been ours. For Suchocki, all this is included in the symbol of "resurrection."[15]

Other questions fall into place within this capacious model. Do we "rise" as the "selves," the *centers of consciousness,* we have come to be during our existence on earth? Do we find ourselves aware of other such centers of consciousness? Suchocki's answer would seem to be that maybe we do. God "feels" our being, she suggests, in relation to God's own eternal goodness and love. But God "feels" us also as we experience ourselves—and even as we have been experienced by others. The "self" each of us is, then, and the "others" with whom that self has known love and hate and betrayal and fulfillment, would enter into the way we participate in God's eternal creativity, justice, and love.[16]

Something like this insight appears in a thought St. Augustine records, in his *Confessions*, concerning a friend who has died. Nebridius, he writes (addressing God), now "drinks your wisdom to the uttermost of his capacity, in happiness without end. Yet I cannot believe that he is so inebriated as to forget me, since you, Lord, from whom he drinks, are mindful of us."[17]

Are "heaven" and "hell" real?

Though the symbols "heaven" and "hell," are often invoked in relation to this life—the hell we make for ourselves, for example, and the hellish conditions unloving people of power can inflict on the powerless—the terms will be used here as intimating possible eternal realities.

"No" to Certain Conceptions of Heaven and Hell

Certain traditional, popular images concerning heaven and hell as beyond-the-world realities need very much to be questioned. That "place up there," for one thing, where angels with harps entertain blissful souls parked on clouds, and that fiery region "down below" (with pitchfork-wielding devils!) reserved for the torment of the faithless dead. Questions also about "getting to" heaven or hell: "Good" people go to heaven, we say, rewarded thus for their moral uprightness; hell is for "bad people"—and serve them right, say too many of us (under our breath).

No, then, to crass images of bliss or bane. No to simplistic quid-pro-quo formulas. "Heaven is not something we get," Joan Chittister insists, "it is something we become."[18] Language locating the dead "up there" or "down there" or "out there" functions simply to suggest their "beyondness"—participating as they do in what must be identified (once again) as the beyondness of God's own reality.

The "no" to heaven always has to do with the "how" of such a mode of being with God and in God. Very different questions are raised, however, about hell, questions as to what such a state could possibly be like and, even more radically, whether there could be a "hell" at all.

The questions have to do most basically with freedom. God is free, we say; and that freedom expresses itself in a love that draws us, and all creation, into fullness of being. Heaven, then, would be God's freely offered gift of eternal life to all who freely receive it. But does the freedom to receive entail a freedom also to reject, entailing a hell of destructive consequences for those who have persistently said "no" to the divine gift? In a dream-vision fantasy about "after-death" states with the title

The Great Divorce, author C. S. Lewis, through the central wisdom figure in the story, remarks of such radical freedom to choose: "There are only two kinds of people in the end: those who say to God, 'Thy will be done,' and those to whom God says, in the end, '*Thy* will be done.'"[19]

The "torment" imagined for such a state, accordingly, would be self-inflicted suffering, the agony of those freely choosing a way which ultimately eats at the very heart of what it is to exist in the "image and likeness of God." This principle also has been dramatized by Lewis, in another fantasy work, already referred to: *The Last Battle*. Central to the action and meaning of this story is a doorway, the doorway, supposedly, to a stable. For the characters in the story presented as having faith, what lies on the other side of that doorway turns out to be Lewis's fantasy version of heaven. The skeptical, self-absorbed Dwarfs, on the other hand (They are "for the Dwarfs" only and they "won't be taken in"), emerge into a "pitch-black, poky, smelly little hole of a stable."[20]

We may want to carry our questioning even further into the realm of "maybe" and ask whether the invitation of divine love *could* ever be so obdurately resisted that the outcome would be total, unending separation from God. Supposing the answer to be "yes," some would then want to ask whether such a one, refusing even that fundamental expression of love by which God sustains all things in being, would not simply pass into nothingness.[21]

And a "Yes," Also, to Heaven?

Yes, heaven is real. As real as God is real. For, as Joan Chittister insists, heaven has to do simply with "the God in whom we live when we die."[22] This is the truth the disciples hear, in that "Farewell Discourse" imagined or reconstructed by the author of the Fourth Gospel, when Jesus declares that he is "returning" to his Father, and will be "preparing a place" so that, at the last, "where [Jesus] is, there [they] may be also."[23]

The imagined conditions of such a life in God include everything previously set down as gifts of creation. So the heaven of Revelation chapters 21-22 is characterized by joyous celebration, loving, peaceable community, fruitfulness, radiant beauty. It is a city—the "new Jerusalem"—but "a river runs through it": the river of the water of life. And the source of that river reminds us, again, why there is a heaven at all; for it flows, we are told, from "the throne of God and of the Lamb."

But if we suppose that we are received into God's eternal life as "selves" and as creatures who have existed in a web of relationships, there could be work yet for us to do, the undertaking suggested by the symbolic term "judgment." Given a dynamic, relational God who takes into "God's time" (eternity) all that we at the end of our time have become, judgment can readily be conceived as a dimension of that process. Within God and, so to speak, "before God," all we have become can be brought under the light of divine truth and into the purifying fire of eternal justice and love.[24]

A brave, lacerating passage from a nightmare-like sequence in T. S. Eliot's "Little Gidding" sets before us the pain and healing such a process could encompass. An aged, weary voice speaks of

> ". . . the rending pain of re-enactment
> Of all that you have done, and been; the shame
> Of motives late revealed, and the awareness
> Of things ill done and done to others' harm
> Which once you took for exercise of virtue. . . .
> From wrong to wrong [the speaker continues] the exasperated spirit
> Proceeds, . . .

[And then comes the one expression of hope for remedy:]

> . . . unless restored by that refining fire
> Where you must move in measure, like a dancer."[25]

Does the Idea of "Purgatory," then, Make Sense?

The "refining fire" spoken of in Eliot's poem refers, of course, to the traditional notion of "Purgatory," the process of purification through which those judged worthy of heaven are gradually prepared for it.

Many in the church—and outside—have found it easy to say "no" to this symbol. History brings to mind some of the abuses that Martin Luther was objecting to, in the protest that eventually created the "Protest-ant" churches—and that a number of contemporary Roman Catholic thinkers repudiate, as well. The selling of "indulgences," especially, whereby gifts to the church—for a pope's fundraising drive, perhaps—could buy prayers which in turn could secure reduced time for souls in Purgatory.

But there may be something to say for the symbol, nevertheless. Entry into God's eternal realm of love and goodness, it has been suggested, entails judgment on "what has been done in the body, whether good or evil"[26] and a divine transformation of all such doings into that which furthers fulfillment in love. Heaven, then, could be envisioned as the "higher reaches," so to speak, in this process of purification and hell as elsewhere along the way.[27]

Progress through such a "purgatory," then, would not be passage toward heaven but *in* heaven. In the "hellish" part of the process, one would not be *in* hell but, as it were, going *through* hell while still within heaven. If heaven is the presence of God, when it is being welcomed as such, the "pain" of a purgatorial process within heaven would be willingly accepted as appropriate to a particular relationship with holy presence. This is why it is said of the personage leaving Dante after their interchange in Canto 26 of the *Purgatorio*: "Then he hid himself in the fire that purifies them."[28]

(Perhaps it would be well to reiterate, at this point, that for a time now our mode of discourse has not been that of an affirming "yes" or a discerning "yes *and* no" but that of a series of reverent but provisional "maybes").

Does the coming of God's "kingdom" bring about the "end of the world"?

The "Kingdom" is a topic so extensive that only a kind of outline can be offered here. Earlier chapters made clear the centrality of this concept in biblical discourse regarding the relations between God and the world. It was pointed out there that:

> The notion of "kingdom," or "rule," celebrates the sovereignty of God our covenant partner as—in the traditional biblical image—"king over all the earth."
>
> The kingdom's having come near was the central theme of Jesus' words and deeds.
>
> The Church is not (as was believed for a time) equivalent to the kingdom of God, but is meant to be an epitome—and a foreshadowing—of the triumph of God's rule.
>
> The rule of God is both a present, ever-forming reality carried on through our responses to the promptings of God's Spirit of justice, compassion, and love, and a vision, still far from fulfillment.

Biblical "Picture Thinking" with regard to God's Kingdom "Come"

The topic of the rule of God reemerges at this point as one of the questions about "last things." Much of the imagery of Holy Scripture and traditional church teaching—imagery powerfully engaging many who follow (and some who strenuously disavow!) the Christian way—has to do with the ultimate future of God's relations with the world.

We read of a Second Coming of Christ—"on the clouds" at the head of angel armies—after a time of unprecedented ordeals for earth-dwellers; of the fall and destruction of the "great whore" Babylon; of a last battle ("Armageddon"), between the forces of Christ and those serving false spiritual powers; of the interim reign—for a "millennium"—of Christ and the martyred saints; of a general resurrection, followed by a final judgment before a "great white throne"; of the destruction, by fire, of the former creation, and the coming to be of "new heavens and new earth"; of a "new Jerusalem" descending to an earth where "righteousness is at home," where "Death will be no more," where the God of covenant faithfulness will be with the people of God forever.[29]

Does This Mean the World Will "Come to an End"?

Among these images of cataclysm and consummation are several that thrust toward us the question: Will the world 'come to an end'? If the answer to that question could be "yes," it would have to be one carefully qualified according to the assumptions governing discourse about "last things."

God is our "end." And so the end is always upon us. For individuals, some aspect of this "end" is brought into view with each relationship confirmed or cut off, each ethical choice made in a career, each life value weakened or reinforced by everyday behavior. And brought up close—for judgment and transformation—when our threescore-and-ten years (give or take) draw near to their closing down.

But the same God who meets individual persons and whole peoples with possibilities for a good ending according to God's "end"—the rule of God in all creation—meets societies and nations and civilizations, also, at transitional end-points along the way. These are times of judgment and possibility—the possibilities diminished sometimes, because of directions lost, wrongs unacknowledged, tragedy ungrieved; augmented at other moments, when prophetic voices have been heeded and creative vision embraced.

Slavery is abolished, Apartheid in South Africa comes to an end, the Berlin wall comes down. The non-violent "politics of the Lamb" (Revelation chapters 4 and 5), and its power of suffering love, win the day. Or—humans slaughter fellow-humans on a scale never seen before, in the "Shoah" bringing degradation and death to millions, in central Africa's genocidal tribal conflict and the ethnic cleansing of the Balkan region. Looking back upon such happenings, the eye of faith can perceive a faithful welcoming, or a ruthless rejection, of gracious possibilities for furthering the rule of God.

As always, language has also to be figured in. Biblical catastrophes and triumphs are often spoken of in end-of-the-world language. Biblical scholar G. B. Caird maintains, for instance, that the cosmic woes incorporated in the discourse attributed to Jesus in Matthew chapter 24—the darkened sun and moon and the stars that begin to fall—point to a later unhappy ending: the destruction of the Jerusalem temple. The chief focus for Jesus' warnings here, Caird argues, is the end not of the world but of an old world *order*.[30]

Even the writings central to all who major in predictions concerning the end have a clear this-worldly reference. Their favorite book, Revelation, was addressed to seven churches (around the end of the first century CE) in a region of what is now western Turkey, its phantasmagoria of images meant to encourage faithful endurance of persecution emanating from Rome (="Babylon") in light of the assurance of God's ultimate triumph.

The earliest followers of Jesus thought of Jesus' resurrection as the "beginning of the end" and of themselves as those "on whom the ends of the ages [had] come."[31] The Jesus who *had* come and (in one or another supernatural manifestation) was yet to come was also understood to be coming to them again and again, from out of the heavenly glory—in their sacred meal the "Lord's Supper," in times of prayer and worship, and in moments of great need, especially that end-of-the-world moment which is the "hour of our death."

The reality—and symbol—of death provides a key whereby the question about *the* "end of the world" can also be answered with a "yes." If dying individuals are received into God's eternal life, for judgment and saving transformation, so too can the world's fullness flow at any moment into the wider experience of God, be brought under judgment, and be transformed into saving possibilities for the future of the world process still ongoing. In this sense, the world comes to an end, in God, at each moment in its history. And, insofar as God's creative, saving work is focused in the crucified-and-risen Jesus, each such moment can be seen as a "second coming" of Christ.

We should not be surprised, then, that the prophetic imagination at work in Holy Scripture presents a heaven that is not centered on individual bliss but on rich communal life—in a city, with streets and trees and a central river, with traffic in and out of its ever-open gates, with commerce and communication.[32] It would seem, at least for any willing to try cautious "maybes," that the symbols of resurrection and heaven—along with those of judgment and final salvation (and "purgatory"?)—can thus take up, as well, the symbol of the kingdom of God and images of a world "coming to an end."

About "last things"—can we also say *"Yes* and I *don't* mean maybe!"?

To the most pressing questions about death, heaven and hell, and the end of the world the response in this chapter has been largely "yes *and* no"—and occasionally (speculatively) "maybe." The question remains: How could we also say "yes" to God, with regard to the issues of faith these concerns imply—"Yes and I *don't* mean maybe"?

We say "yes" to the *reign of God* by praying (as in the Lord's Prayer) for its coming, working for its actualization here and now, and hoping for its fulfillment in God's eternity.

Living in hope is not like solving an algebraic equation, so much on this side (resources, gifts, hard work) automatically yielding equivalent outcomes (change for the better) on the other side. Nor is hope the same thing as optimism, that generalized expectation that "things will turn out OK." We need only recall Jesus pleading with God in the Garden, or standing on trial before the Roman governor, to realize, instead, that our hope, that "sure and steadfast anchor of the soul,"[33] has to be in God.

In God—not in systems or programs or leaders but in the eternal presence and power that welcomes, and judges, and can finally redeem all things, no matter how fleeting and fragmentary or how massive and enduring. The Bible's "picture thinking" concerning "last things" affirms what the Lord's Prayer assumes—that the will of God people of faith strive to actualize "on earth" is ultimately "done . . . in heaven."

And how do we say "yes" to *heaven*? Again, by hoping for heaven—directing this hope, as well, to God. For the ground for such hope is not some estimate of our own worthiness of heavenly bliss nor our own imaginings of that mode of being which (as Paul reminds us) "God has prepared for those who love him."[34]

But we do also offer this "yes" by way of imagination. Keeping in mind that it is all "picture thinking," we do well to revel in the wealth of images and ideas of heaven provided by fragments from Jesus' teaching and, most lavishly of all, by much of the Book of Revelation. These can provide an authentic opening on some shimmer of an aura, some touch of ineffable harmony, that says: This is what it is like (in Paul's words) "to be with the Lord forever."[35]

We say "yes" to heaven "there," finally, by living heaven *here*—and saying a vehement "no" to anything that can, for any one of God's creatures, make earthly life a "hell." Dorothy Day, co-founder of the Catholic Worker movement, was one who gave herself to alleviating the hellish sufferings of certain on-earth inner-city dwellers, but who spoke of heaven as well, reminding us that "all the way to heaven is heaven."[36]

When are we on that heavenly way? Whenever, first of all, we are savoring the gifts, described in earlier chapters, that are ours as creatures of God. Whenever we allow ourselves (with poet-prophet William Blake) "to see a world in a grain of sand / And a heaven in a wild flower." Whenever fine music and poetry are ringing in our ears or in our minds (The great twentieth-century theologian Karl Barth declared that Mozart was the person he expected to greet first in heaven). Whenever we are being members one of another, welcoming one another "just as Christ has welcomed [us]."[37] And whenever we join in ordered worship, participate in that Supper in which (according to Scripture) we "proclaim the Lord's death until he comes,"[38] and enter into solitary prayer and meditation.

Can we even come to say "yes and I *don't* mean maybe"—to raise this personal end-of-the-world question yet again—to the God who meets us in our *dying*? Here our guide is none other than the one through whose death and rising again we find liberation from what enslaves us and reconciliation with that from which we have been estranged. Help can be found in some of the "last words" ascribed to Jesus.

A word from the cross given in John offers a dying "yes" to what has been and is now coming to an end. For just before "[giving] up his spirit" Jesus says, concerning the "work" God had given him to do: "It is finished." Transposing into psychological terms, might we understand *our* final life task as—in Erik Erikson's formulation—one of maintaining "ego integrity" over against the temptation to despair?[39]

Mark and Matthew present a word that is shockingly different. Their account of the crucifixion has Jesus calling out, in the unnatural darkness of early afternoon, "My God, my God, why have you forsaken me?"[40] That cry—the opening sentence of the sustained lament that is Psalm 22—conveys not just the terror of one facing death but something even more lacerating: a feeling of abandonment, a sense of God as, in this moment, an absence rather than a presence.

But there is hurtful help in these words as well. For we who must die need to realize that we have no assurance of dying "a good death."[41] We need to be able to say "yes" even to panic and utter aloneness, knowing that such desolation has entered the divine life, in Jesus, and is part of what God is compassionately willing to receive, with us, in our passing over.

One more word, this one, again, from Luke chapter 23 and—once more—an echo from a Psalm: "Father, into your hands I commend my spirit."[42] I cannot hear these words without recalling a decisive confrontation with the issue of my own dying.

> I was at the lectern in the church I was attending at the time, reading a passage from Romans chapter 14. I had failed, this time, to go through the reading in advance, and so I was reading it "cold."
>
> After some verses of little relevance to my life or that of my hearers, I found myself saying words of great import, indeed.
>
> "We do not live to ourselves [I read], and we do not die to ourselves. If we live, we live to the Lord, and if we die, we die to the Lord; so then, whether we live or whether we die, we are the Lord's."
>
> It was as if, suddenly, something turned over in me. I stopped for a moment, before reading on. And I sensed, there and then, that some perplexity concerning my own thoughts of death, and fear of dying, had been to some degree resolved. Resolved forever—even though, when the time comes, I may well make my exit kicking and screaming like so many others!

We learn to say "yes" to our own dying as we deepen in our "yes" to God—to the divine presence we meet as self-revealing mystery, creator and preserver of all that is, covenant partner and companion, reconciling and liberating savior, and (ultimately) source and hope of eternal life. We learn that "yes" as we participate in the Spirit of the Jesus who died and who "rose again" and is alive forevermore, in whom "death no longer has dominion."[43]

These words are being written, as it happens, in the afternoon of an Easter Day early in a new century and a new millennium. The blessing of Easter assurance! deriving from the belief that God is real—the God present incomparably in Jesus Christ—and that heaven, therefore, is also real. It is in that yes-and-I-*don't*-mean-maybe faith that we can learn to say, with the dying Jesus—at every moment along the way as well as when our end is upon us—"Into your hands I commend my spirit."

ENDNOTES

[1] Ian T. Ramsey, *Christian Discourse: Some Logical Explorations* (London: Oxford University Press, 1965), 57.

[2] *The Confessions of St. Augustine,* trans. Maria Boulding, O.S.B. (New York: Vintage Books, 1998), 319.

[3] C. S. Lewis, *The Last Battle* (New York: Macmillan, 1956), 173.

[4] William Shakespeare, *The Tempest,* Act V, scene 1.

[5] James William McClendon, Jr., *Systematic Theology: Doctrine, Volume II* (Nashville: Abingdon Press, 1994), 75-77.

[6] References are to: 2 Kings 2:11; Isaiah 11:6-9; Matthew 26:64; Dante Alighieri, "Inferno," *The Divine Comedy,* trans. Charles S. Singleton (Princeton, N.J.: Princeton University Press, 1973), Canto 34; Revelation chapters 21-22.

[7] Popular media can be especially misleading in this regard. A runup-to-the-millennium feature in *Newseek,* for instance (in the November 1, 1999 issue), promises to present "*what the Bible says* about the end of the world" (emphasis mine); and then, from the Bible's muster of end-time imagery, simply "rounds up the usual suspects."

[8] McClendon, 66.

[9] The comparison is that of the nineteenth-century philosopher Emmanuel Feuerbach; cited in Karl Rahner, *Foundations of Christian Faith: An Introduction to the Idea of Christianity,* trans. William V. Dych (New York: Seabury Press, 1978), 436.

[10] Immortality as a way of envisaging life beyond death came into Christian thought mainly through the influence of certain Greek philosophers (most notably Plato) on various theologians of the Church. The survival of an "immortal soul" continues to be, for many people, the dominant model for understanding "life after death."

[11] The most prominent Old Testament reference is Daniel 12:2: "Many of those who sleep in the dust of the earth shall awake, some to everlasting life, and some to shame and everlasting contempt."

[12] Revelation 1:17-18.

[13] 2 Corinthians 4:14.

[14] References are to Revelation 20:4b-5; 1 Thessalonians 4:17; 2 Corinthians 5:8.

[15] Marjorie Hewitt Suchocki, *God—Christ—Church: A Practical Guide to Process Theology,* rev. ed. (New York: Crossroad, 1989),199ff.

[16] Suchocki, 205-206, 210.

[17] *Confessions of St. Augustine,* 174.

[18] Joan Chittister, *In Search of Belief* (Liguori, Missouri: Liguori/Triumph, 1999), 49.

[19] C. S. Lewis, *The Great Divorce* (New York: Macmillan, 1955), 69.

[20] Lewis, *The Last Battle,* 140, 133.

[21] Such a possibility is put forward, e.g., in John Macquarrie, *Principles of Christian Theology,* 2nd ed. (New York: Charles Scribner's Sons, 1977), 366-67; and Hans Kung, *Eternal Life? Life after Death as a Medical, Philosophical, and Theological Problem,* trans. Edward Quinn (Garden City, NY: Doubleday and Co., 1984), 140.

[22] Chittister, 52.

[23] John 14:2-3.

[24] Suchocki, 210-13.

[25] T. S. Eliot, *Four Quartets,* "Little Gidding," in *The Complete Poems and Plays 1909-1950* (New York: Harcourt, Brace and Co., 1952), 142.

[26] 2 Corinthians 5:10.

[27] The idea is that of philosopher of religion John Hick, in *The Westminster Dictionary of Christian Theology,* ed. Alan Richardson and John Bowden (Philadelphia: Westminster Press, 1983), 333. It presupposes "a continued person-making process in other spheres beyond this world" and an understanding of heaven as "unending

movement through the infinite dimensions of God's creativity."

Elsewhere, Hick ventures even further afield in the territory of "maybe." Borrowing from Hindu and Buddhist ideas of reincarnation, he suggests that the "how" whereby heaven unfolds within the eternal reality of divine love and justice could entail a *series* of lives, each a transitional phase of our life in God. *Death and Eternal Life* (San Francisco: Harper and Row, 1976), 414ff.

[28] Dante, "Purgatorio," *The Divine Comedy*, trans. Charles S. Singleton (Princeton, N.J.: Princeton University Press, 1973), 289.

[29] References are to Matthew 26:64; Revelation 7:14, Revelation chapters 17-18; 16:14-16, with 19:11-21; 20:4-6; 2 Peter 3:12-13, with Revelation 21:1-4.

[30] George Bradford Caird, *The Language and Imagery of the Bible* (Grand Rapids, Michigan: Eerdmans, 1997), 259, 266.

[31] 1 Corinthians 10:11.

[32] Revelation 21:22-26; 22:1-5.

[33] Hebrews 6:19.

[34] 1 Corinthians 2:9-10.

[35] 1 Thessalonians 4:17. A rich resource for surveying the imagery of heaven is *The Book of Heaven: An Anthology of Writings from Ancient to Modern Times*, ed. Carol Zaleski and Philip Zaleski (New York: Oxford University Press, 2000).

[36] Cited in McClendon, *Doctrine*, 102. Earlier reference, relating this remark to the saying of Catherine of Siena: "Heaven can begin here," in *Systematic Theology, Vol. I, Ethics* (Nashville: Abingdon Press, 1986), 296.

[37] Romans 15:7.

[38] 1 Corinthians 11:26

[39] John 19:30. Erik H. Erikson, in *Childhood and Society*, rev. ed. (Harmondsworth, Middlesex, England: Penguin Books, 1965), 260, describes this last life passage as "the acceptance of one's one and only life cycle as something that had to be . . . ."

[40] Mark 15:34.

[41] Sherwin B. Nuland, *How We Die: Reflections on Life's Final Chapter* (New York: Alfred A. Knopf, 1994), xvi, 264-65.

[42] Luke 23:46; Psalm 31:5.

[43] Romans 6:9.

www.ingramcontent.com/pod-product-compliance
Lightning Source LLC
LaVergne TN
LVHW050647100826
845148LV00011B/2019

* 9 7 8 1 5 9 7 5 2 0 5 8 4 *